SPECTRUM

TEXAS
Test Prep

SPECTRUM

Frank Schaffer Publications®

Spectrum is an imprint of Frank Schaffer Publications.

Printed in the United States of America. All rights reserved. Except as permitted under the United States Copyright Act, no part of this publication may be reproduced or distributed in any form or by any means, or stored in a database or retrieval system, without prior written permission from the publisher, unless otherwise indicated. Frank Schaffer Publications is an imprint of School Specialty Children's Publishing. Copyright © 2004 School Specialty Children's Publishing.

Send all inquiries to:
Frank Schaffer Publications
3195 Wilson Drive NW
Grand Rapids, Michigan 49544

ISBN 0-7696-3023-5

3 4 5 6 7 8 9 10 PHXBK 09 08 07 06 05 04

Table of Contents

What's Inside?

This workbook is designed to help you and your third-grader understand what he or she will be expected to know on the Texas third-grade state tests. The testing program, called the Texas Assessment of Knowledge and Skills (TAKS), measures student learning in different subject areas,

Practice Pages

The workbook is divided into a Language Arts section and Mathematics section. Each section has practice activities that have questions similar to those that will appear on the state tests. Students should use a pencil to fill in the correct answers and to complete any writing on these activities.

Texas Content Standards

Before each practice section is a list of the state standards covered by that section. The shaded "What it means" sections will help to explain any information in the standards that might be unfamiliar.

Mini-Tests and Final Tests

Practice activities are grouped by state standard. When each group is completed the student can move on to a Mini-Test that covers the material presented on those practice activities. After an entire set of standards and accompanying activities are completed, the student should take the Final Tests, which incorporate materials from all the practice activities in that section.

Final Test Answer Sheet

The Final Tests have a separate answer sheet that mimics the style of the answer sheet the students will use on the state tests. The answer sheet appears at the end of each Final Test.

How Am I Doing?

The **How Am I Doing?** pages are designed to help students identify areas where they are proficient and areas where they still need more practice. Students can keep track of each of their Mini-Test scores on these pages.

Answer Key

Answers to all the practice activities, mini-tests, and final tests are listed by page number and appear at the end of the book.

What kinds of information does my child have to know to pass the test?

The Texas Education Agency provides a list of the knowledge and skills that students are expected to master at each grade level. The practice activities in this workbook provide students with practice in each of these areas.

Are there special strategies or tips that will help my child do well?

The workbook provides sample questions that have content similar to that on the state tests. Test-taking tips are offered throughout the book.

How do I know what areas my child needs help in?

A special How Am I Doing? section will help you and your third-grader evaluate progress. It will pinpoint areas where more work is needed as well as areas where your student excels.

TAKS Reading
Content Standards

The reading section of the state test measures knowledge in four different areas.

1) *Objective 1: Basic understanding of written texts*

       Reading/word identification

       Reading/variety of texts

       Reading/vocabulary development

       Reading/comprehension

2) *Objective 2: Applying knowledge of literary elements to understand written texts*

       Reading/text structures/literary concepts

3) *Objective 3: Using a variety of strategies to analyze written texts*

       Reading/comprehension

       Reading/text structures/literary concepts

4) *Objective 4: Applying critical-thinking skills to analyze written texts*

       Reading/comprehension

       Reading/literary response

Reading
Table of Contents

TAKS Reading—Objective 1

The student will demonstrate a basic understanding of culturally diverse written texts.

(3.5) Reading/word identification
The student uses a variety of word identification strategies. The student is expected to
(D) use root words and other structural cues such as prefixes, suffixes, and derivational endings to recognize words (3); and *(See pages 8–9.)*
(E) use knowledge of word order (syntax) and context to support word identification and confirm word meaning (1–3). *(See pages 10–11.)*

What it means:
- Students should be able to look at familiar words in a sentence or a passage to help them find the meaning of unknown words.
- Students should recognize the meaning of common word beginnings, or prefixes, such as *un-*, *re-*, and *pre-*, and suffixes, such as *-er*, *-est*, and *-ful*. They can use this knowledge to determine the meaning of unknown words.

(3.7) Reading/variety of texts
The student reads widely for different purposes in varied sources. The student is expected to
(B) read from a variety of genres [for pleasure and] to acquire information [from both print and electronic sources] (2–3). *(See pages 12–13.)*

What it means:
- Genre is the type or category of literature. Some examples of genres include fiction, biographies, poetry, and fables. Each genre is characterized by various differences in form. For example, the fable differs from the broader category of fiction because it has a moral or character lesson.

(3.8) Reading/vocabulary development
The student develops an extensive vocabulary. The student is expected to
(C) use [resources and references such as beginners' dictionaries, glossaries, available technology, and] context to build word meanings and to confirm pronunciations of words (2–3); and *(See pages 14–15.)*
(D) demonstrate knowledge of synonyms, antonyms, and multi-meaning words [for example, by sorting, classifying, and identifying related words] (3). *(See pages 16–17.)*

What it means:
- Synonyms are words that mean the same or about the same as each other. For example, *jump* and *hop* are synonyms.
- Antonyms are words that are the opposite or nearly opposite of each other. For example, *above* and *below* are antonyms.
- Multi-meaning words are words that spelled the same, but have different meanings. For example, *long* can mean both "to desire" and "not short."

(3.9) Reading/comprehension
The student uses a variety of strategies to comprehend selections read aloud and selections read independently. The student is expected to
(C) retell [or act out the order of] important events in stories (K–3); and *(See pages 18–19.)*
(H) produce summaries of text selections (2–3). *(See pages 20–21.)*

Reading/Word Identification

Objective 1

Expectation: use root words and other structural cues such as prefixes, suffixes, and derivational endings to recognize words

Example:

Find the word in which only the prefix is underlined.

- (F) <u>pre</u>view
- (G) <u>d</u>ecide
- (H) <u>a</u>lert
- (J) mon<u>ster</u>

Answer: (F)

DIRECTIONS: Choose the best answer.

1. Find the word in which only the suffix is underlined.
   - (A) bun<u>dle</u>
   - (B) mo<u>stly</u>
   - (C) run<u>ner</u>
   - (D) jump<u>ing</u>

2. Find the word in which only the prefix is underlined.
   - (F) <u>pre</u>tend
   - (G) <u>al</u>low
   - (H) <u>be</u>tween
   - (J) <u>un</u>known

3. Find the word in which only the suffix is underlined.
   - (A) land<u>ed</u>
   - (B) clos<u>et</u>
   - (C) stor<u>ms</u>
   - (D) tele<u>vision</u>

4. Which of these words does not have a suffix?
   - (F) runner
   - (G) untie
   - (H) hairless
   - (J) washable

5. Which of these words does not have a prefix?
   - (A) defrost
   - (B) nonstop
   - (C) fixable
   - (D) prepay

6. What does the prefix *un-* mean in the word *unsafe*?
   - (F) over
   - (G) not
   - (H) in favor of
   - (J) before

GO

Reading/Word Identification

Objective 1

Expectation: *use root words and other structural cues such as prefixes, suffixes, and derivational endings to recognize words*

---

7. **What does the suffix *-less* mean in the word *hopeless*?**

   (A) full of

   (B) like

   (C) place

   (D) without

8. **Find the word in which only the root word is underlined.**

   (F) <u>carp</u>et

   (H) barr<u>el</u>

   (G) <u>play</u>ful

   (J) <u>re</u>lease

9. **Find the word in which only the root word is underlined.**

   (A) <u>old</u>er

   (B) <u>un</u>safe

   (C) roo<u>my</u>

   (D) full<u>y</u>

10. **Find the word that means "to play again."**

    (F) playful

    (G) replay

    (H) player

    (J) display

11. **Find the word that means "not safe."**

    (A) safest

    (B) safely

    (C) unsafe

    (D) safety

12. **Which of the following words means "to see beforehand"?**

    (F) bifocal

    (G) microscope

    (H) present

    (J) preview

13. **Which of the following words means "to let go"?**

    (A) release

    (B) restore

    (C) reflect

    (D) regain

14. **Which of the following words means "cautious"?**

    (F) careless

    (G) careful

    (H) uncaring

    (J) quick

STOP

9

Name _____   Date _____

Reading/Word Identification

Objective 1

Expectation: use knowledge of word order (syntax) and context to support word identification and confirm word meaning

 Clue The meaning of the sentence will give you a clue about which answer to choose.

DIRECTIONS: Choose the best answer.

1. My mother used the garden _____ to wash the dog.
   - (A) rake
   - (B) seeds
   - (C) hose
   - (D) gate

2. The _____ ride on the roller coaster made us yell out loud.
   - (F) interesting
   - (G) boring
   - (H) slow
   - (J) thrilling

3. The stormy weather will _____ all night.
   - (A) change
   - (B) continue
   - (C) stop
   - (D) knock

4. You should _____ this idea.
   - (F) think
   - (G) drive
   - (H) consider
   - (J) write

DIRECTIONS: Find the word that means the same thing as the underlined word.

5. Are you starting on your <u>journey</u>?
   Journey means—
   - (A) class
   - (B) lesson
   - (C) trip
   - (D) vacation

6. Please bring me <u>Volume</u> K of the encyclopedia.
   Volume means—
   - (F) amount
   - (G) book
   - (H) measurement
   - (J) large

7. His grades have <u>improved</u>.
   Improved means—
   - (A) gotten better
   - (B) gotten worse
   - (C) fixed
   - (D) painted

GO

Reading/Word Identification

Objective 1

Expectation: use knowledge of word order (syntax) and context to support word identification and confirm word meaning

---

8. Tara's <u>excuse</u> was a good one.
   Excuse means—

   (F) dismiss

   (G) forgive

   (H) explanation

   (J) forgotten

9. The dog seemed <u>fearless</u> as it raced into the crashing waves.
   Fearless means—

   (A) happy

   (B) sincere

   (C) angry

   (D) unafraid

10. The house was heated by <u>solar</u> energy.
    Solar means—

    (F) electric

    (G) water

    (H) sun-powered

    (J) gas

11. The roofer used an <u>extension</u> ladder to fix the shingles.
    Extension means—

    (A) rolling

    (B) expandable

    (C) heavy

    (D) permanent

DIRECTIONS: Find the sentence in which the underlined word is used in the same way.

12. The <u>field</u> is planted with corn.

    (F) The field of technology is constantly changing.

    (G) We can see deer in the field by our house.

    (H) Her field is nursing.

    (J) Our field trip is next thursday.

13. The <u>general</u> idea was to weave a basket.

    (A) She is a general in the army.

    (B) The soldiers followed their general into battle.

    (C) I think that the general had the best idea.

    (D) No general study of history can cover everything.

14. Brake pads are made at a <u>plant</u> in our city.

    (F) The most beautiful plant is a rose.

    (G) Plant your feet and don't move.

    (H) Farmers plant crops.

    (J) My uncle worked at the plant.

STOP

Name _____ Date _____

Reading/Variety of Texts

Objective 1

Expectation: read from a variety of genres [for pleasure and] to acquire information [from both print and electronic sources]

DIRECTIONS: Read the passage and answer the questions.

Lunch Guests

It was a sunny spring day. Kaye and her friend Tasha were walking in the woods. As they walked, they noticed many squirrels ahead of them running in the same direction.

"Let's follow them and see where they are going," said Tasha.

"Great idea!" exclaimed Kaye, and the two girls raced ahead.

Soon they came to a large clearing in the forest. There were hundreds and hundreds of squirrels—more squirrels than either girl had ever seen. As they stared in amazement at the scene before them, a plump gray squirrel with a fluffy tail skittered over to them and said politely, "Would you care to join us for lunch?"

Tasha and Kaye were stunned into silence. But after a moment, they looked at each other, shrugged, and said, "Why not?" They both liked nuts.

1. **This passage is which genre (type) of literature?**
   - (A) poetry
   - (B) fiction
   - (C) biography
   - (D) fable

2. **What clues in the story helped you decide what genre it is?**
   - (F) Real squirrels can't talk.
   - (G) The girls raced.
   - (H) Squirrels like nuts.
   - (J) It was a sunny spring day.

3. **This genre is usually about _____.**
   - (A) the life of a real person
   - (B) how something came to be the way it is
   - (C) how to do something
   - (D) made-up places and events

4. **The purpose of this genre is usually to _____.**
   - (F) entertain the reader
   - (G) alarm the reader
   - (H) inform the reader
   - (J) challenge the reader

Reading/Variety of Texts

Objective 1

Expectation: *read from a variety of genres [for pleasure and] to acquire information [from both print and electronic sources]*

Quicksand

Stories of people and animals sinking into quicksand have been told for hundreds of years. Although some of the stories may be true, it helps to understand what quicksand really is.

Quicksand is a deep bed of light, loose sand that is full of water. On the surface it looks much like regular sand, but it is really very different. Regular sand is packed firmly and can be walked on. Because quicksand is loose and full of water, it cannot support much weight.

Quicksand usually develops around rivers and lakes. Water collects in the sand and does not drain away. It continues to collect until the sand becomes soft.

Although some objects can float in quicksand, it cannot support the heavy weight of an animal or person.

---

5. This passage is which genre (type) of literature?

- (A) poetry
- (B) biography
- (C) fable
- (D) nonfiction

6. What clues in the passage helped you decide what genre it is?

- (F) It is based on stories from hundreds of years ago.
- (G) Facts about quicksand are given.
- (H) There is an animal in the picture.
- (J) Quicksand forms around tall buildings.

7. The purpose of this genre is usually to _____ .

- (A) entertain the reader
- (B) alarm the reader
- (C) inform the reader
- (D) challenge the reader

8. This genre usually includes _____ .

- (F) accurate information
- (G) cartoon characters
- (H) stage directions
- (J) words that rhyme

STOP

Reading/Vocabulary Development

Objective 1

Expectation: use [resources and references such as beginners' dictionaries, glossaries, available technology, and] context to build word meanings and to confirm pronunciations of words

Clue Remember, dictionary entries can tell you more than just the meaning of a word. They also can help you say a word correctly and tell you if a word is a noun, verb, adjective, adverb, or pronoun.

DIRECTIONS: Use the dictionary entries to answer numbers 1–3.

save [sāv] *v.* **1.** to rescue from harm or danger. **2.** to keep in a safe condition. **3.** to set aside for future use; store. **4.** to avoid.

saving [sā´vĭng] *n.* **1.** rescuing from harm or danger. **2.** avoiding excess spending; economy. **3.** something saved.

savory [sā´və-rē] *adj.* **1.** appealing to the taste or smell. **2.** salty to the taste.

1. **The *a* in the word *saving* sounds most like the word _____ .**
   - (A) pat
   - (B) ape
   - (C) heated
   - (D) naughty

2. **Which sentence uses *save* in the same way as definition number 3?**
   - (F) Firefighters save lives.
   - (G) She saves half of all she earns.
   - (H) Going by jet saves eight hours of driving.
   - (J) The life jacket saved the boy from drowning.

3. **Which sentence uses *savory* in the same way as definition number 2?**
   - (A) The savory stew made me thirsty.
   - (B) The savory bank opened an account.
   - (C) This flower has a savory scent.
   - (D) The savory dog rescued me.

DIRECTIONS: Use the dictionary entry to answer numbers 4 and 5.

beam [bēm] *n.* **1.** a squared-off log used to support a building. **2.** a ray of light. **3.** the wooden roller in a loom. *v.* **1.** to shine. **2.** to smile broadly.

4. **Which use of the word *beam* is a verb?**
   - (F) The beam held up the plaster ceiling.
   - (G) The beam of sunlight warmed the room.
   - (H) She moved the beam before she added a row of wool.
   - (J) The bright stars beam in the night sky.

GO

Reading/Vocabulary Development

Objective 1

Expectation: *use [resources and references such as beginners' dictionaries, glossaries, available technology, and] context to build word meanings and to confirm pronunciations of words*

5. **Which sentence uses the word *beam* in the same way as the first definition of the noun?**
   - (A) The ceiling beam had fallen into the room.
   - (B) The beam of the loom was broken.
   - (C) She beamed her approval.
   - (D) The beam of sunlight came through the tree.

6. **The *ea* in the word *beam* sounds most like the word _____ .**
   - (F) red
   - (G) seem
   - (H) tense
   - (J) penny

DIRECTIONS: Use the definitions on the right to answer the questions.

7. **How do you spell the word that means "a method of self-defense"?**
   - (A) karete
   - (B) kurate
   - (C) kerate
   - (D) karate

8. **How do you spell the word that means "coins and bills used as money"?**
   - (F) currency
   - (G) curency
   - (H) currincy
   - (J) currencie

9. **Which word best fits in the sentence, "When will Agnes _____ from her cold"?**
   - (A) nutrition
   - (B) celebrate
   - (C) fox
   - (D) recover

currency

Coins and bills used as money are <u>currency</u>.

karate

<u>Karate</u> is a method of self-defense invented in Japan.

recover

To <u>recover</u> is to get better after being sick.

STOP

Reading/Vocabulary Development

Objective 1

Expectation: demonstrate knowledge of synonyms, antonyms, and multi-meaning words [for example, by sorting, classifying, and identifying related words]

DIRECTIONS: Read the passage and answer the questions.

The Great Ice Age

Long ago, the climate of Earth began to cool. As the temperature dropped, giant sheets of ice, called glaciers, moved across the land. As time went on, snow and ice covered many forests and grasslands.

Some plants and animals could not survive the changes in the climate. Other animals moved to warmer land. But some animals were able to adapt. They learned to live with the cold and snowy weather.

Finally, Earth's temperature began to rise. The ice and snow began to melt. Today, the land at the North and South Poles is a reminder of the Great Ice Age.

1. **Which of the following is an antonym for melt?**
   - (A) thaw
   - (B) freeze
   - (C) fix
   - (D) order

2. **Which of the following is a synonym for climate?**
   - (F) weather
   - (G) rain
   - (H) crumble
   - (J) last

3. **Which of the following is an antonym for rise?**
   - (A) stay
   - (B) go
   - (C) fall
   - (D) happen

4. **Which of the following is a synonym for adapt?**
   - (F) change
   - (G) remain
   - (H) move
   - (J) survive

GO

Reading/Vocabulary Development

Objective 1

Expectation: demonstrate knowledge of synonyms, antonyms, and multi-meaning words [for example, by sorting, classifying, and identifying related words]

5. **Which of the following is an antonym for remind?**

   (A) again

   (B) forget

   (C) help

   (D) change

6. **Which of the following is a synonym for grasslands?**

   (F) prairie

   (G) ocean

   (H) dessert

   (J) mountains

7. **Which word can mean "to desire" and "not short"?**

   (A) cool

   (B) earth

   (C) long

   (D) ago

8. **Which word can mean "to come to rest" and "the part of earth that is not water"?**

   (F) land

   (G) rise

   (H) long

   (J) weather

DIRECTIONS: For each pair of words or phrases, put an **S** if they are synonyms and an **A** if they are antonyms.

9. _____ giant sheet of ice   glacier

10. _____ survive   die

11. _____ warm   cool

12. _____ giant   huge

13. _____ dropped   fell

14. _____ temperature   measure of heat or cold

15. _____ grasslands   prairie

16. _____ remind   forget

17. _____ melt   freeze

18. _____ climate   weather

19. _____ rise   fall

20. _____ adapt   learn to live with

STOP

Reading/Comprehension

Objective 1

Expectation: retell [or act out the order of] important events in stories

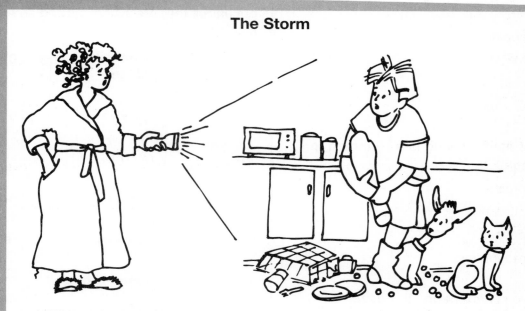

The Storm

Willie sat in front of the TV while a storm raged outside his house. The wind howled, the rain came down in buckets, and thunder boomed loudly. The high winds knocked down a huge oak tree down the street. The tree fell on top of the street's power line, cutting the electricity to Willie's house. Willie found a flashlight and turned it on.

Willie shone the flashlight ahead of him as he walked down the hallway. As he entered the kitchen, the flashlight batteries died. The room became inky black. Willie ran into the wall and stubbed his toe. He hollered and jumped on one foot. He bumped into the table, which knocked over his marble jar. Marbles scattered all over the table and floor.

Muttsie, Willie's dog, jumped up at the noise and ran toward Willie's voice. The dog skidded on the marbles. She flew across the floor into her dog dishes, spilling water and food everywhere.

Willie's cat, Kitty, was showered with water from the spilled dog dish. She jumped to the safety of the counter. She landed on the edge of a cookie sheet sticking out of the dish rack. The cookie sheet flipped over, taking the contents of the dish rack with it. The pots, plates, and silverware crashed to the floor, making an awful racket. One of the pans struck the flour canister. The flour poofed up, covering everything in white.

Willie's mother heard the noise and came running with another flashlight. Amazed, she walked into the kitchen and stopped. "What happened here?" she asked.

GO →

Reading/Comprehension

Objective 1

Expectation: retell [or act out the order of] important events in stories

---

DIRECTIONS: Use the information in the passage to answer the following questions.

1. **What caused the electricity to be cut off to Willie's house?**

   (A) The storm blew down the oak tree.

   (B) Willie ran into the wall.

   (C) The house was dark.

   (D) Willie found a flashlight.

2. **Which of these gives the events in the correct order?**

   (F) Willie ran into the wall and stubbed his toe, then the flashlight batteries died.

   (G) Willie bumped into the table, then he ran into the wall and stubbed his toe.

   (H) Willie knocked over his marble jar, then he ran into the wall and stubbed his toe.

   (J) The flashlight batteries died, then Willie ran into the wall and stubbed his toe.

3. **What caused Muttsie to spill the water and food?**

   (A) Muttsie bumped into the table, spilling the marbles.

   (B) Muttsie skidded on the marbles.

   (C) Muttsie flipped over the cookie sheet.

   (D) Muttsie jumped to the safety of the counter.

4. **Which of these events happened first?**

   (F) Kitty jumped to the safety of the counter.

   (G) The cookie sheet flipped over.

   (H) Kitty was showered with water.

   (J) Kitty landed on the edge of a cookie sheet.

5. **How did everything end up covered in flour?**

   (A) Willie knocked over the flour canister.

   (B) Willie's mother bumped into the table.

   (C) One of the pans from the dish rack struck the flour canister.

   (D) Muttsie bumped into the table.

6. **When Willie's mother saw the mess she was _____ .**

   (F) happy

   (G) thrilled

   (H) amazed

   (J) angry

STOP

Reading/Comprehension

Objective
1

Expectation: *produce summaries of text selections*

Native American Biographies

Wilma Mankiller

Wilma Mankiller was born in 1945. She is a Cherokee from Oklahoma. Mankiller lived in San Francisco for a long time before returning to Oklahoma. In San Francisco, she learned many skills that could help her as a chief. She became Principal Chief of the Cherokee Nation in 1985. She has worked hard for improved health care, civil rights, and many other important causes. Mankiller believes in an old Cherokee saying about being of good mind. She says that today this is called "positive thinking."

Crazy Horse

A fierce warrior, Crazy Horse was known as a Sioux who would not give up. Born in 1849, Crazy Horse worked hard to keep the Native American way of life from disappearing. He did not want to lose the customs of his people. Most people say that Crazy Horse did not allow pictures to be taken of him, as this was against his beliefs. His image, though, is carved in a mountain at the Crazy Horse Memorial in South Dakota.

Chief Joseph

Born in 1840, Chief Joseph was given a Native American name that meant *Thunder Rolling Down the Mountain*. Joseph became chief of the Nez Percé. There were many attempts to force Chief Joseph's group onto a small Idaho reservation. At first, Chief Joseph refused to go. Then he recognized that the military would force him and his people onto the reservation anyway. Chief Joseph wanted peace for his people, so he surrendered to the military.

Red Cloud

Many believe that Red Cloud was one of the most important Sioux chiefs of the nineteenth century. Born in 1822, Red Cloud became a great leader helping to hold and gain land for the Sioux. Red Cloud's work and the plans that he made to help his people were quite successful. As a result, the United States entered into a treaty that forced the United States to abandon all of its forts in one area. The treaty also promised that the Sioux could keep a great amount of their land.

Wilma Mankiller

Crazy Horse

Chief Joseph

Red Cloud

GO

Reading/Comprehension

Objective
1

Expectation: *produce summaries of text selections*

DIRECTIONS: Use the information in the biographies to answer the questions.

1. **Which of the following best summarizes the biography of Wilma Mankiller?**

   (A) Chief Wilma Mankiller worked for improved health care and civil rights for the Cherokee.

   (B) Mankiller believes in an old Cherokee saying about being of good mind.

   (C) Wilma Mankiller was born in 1945.

   (D) Mankiller lived in San Francisco for a long time before returning to Oklahoma.

2. **Which of the following best summarizes the biography of Crazy Horse?**

   (F) Crazy Horse was known as a Sioux who would not give up.

   (G) There is now a Crazy Horse Memorial in South Dakota.

   (H) Crazy Horse worked hard to keep the Native American way of life from disappearing.

   (J) Crazy Horse did not allow pictures to be taken of him.

3. **Which of the following best summarizes the biography of Chief Joseph?**

   (A) Chief Joseph surrendered to the military.

   (B) Chief Joseph, wanted peace for the Nez Percé.

   (C) Chief Joseph was born in 1840.

   (D) Chief Joseph's Native American name meant *Thunder Rolling Down the Mountain*.

4. **Which of the following best summarizes the biography of Red Cloud?**

   (F) The United States entered into a treaty with Red Cloud.

   (G) Red Cloud's work was quite successful.

   (H) Red Cloud was born in 1822.

   (J) Red Cloud became a great leader, helping to hold and gain land for the Sioux.

STOP

Objective

1

Mini-Test

DIRECTIONS: Read the passage, then answer the questions.

A Microscope

Have you ever looked into a microscope? A microscope is an <u>instrument</u> that helps us see very small things by <u>magnifying</u> them. Scientists and doctors can use microscopes to study parts of the body, such as blood and skin cells. They can also study germs, tiny plants, and tiny animals.

1. In this passage, what does the word *instrument* mean?

- (A) a tool
- (B) a drum
- (C) an office
- (D) a paper

2. In this passage, what does the word *magnifying* mean?

- (F) making them smaller
- (G) making them larger
- (H) making them red
- (J) making them disappear

3. Which of these best summarizes the passage?

- (A) A microscope helps us see small things by magnifying them.
- (B) A microscope helps us see blood cells.
- (C) A microscope is an instrument.
- (D) A microscope helps doctors and scientists.

DIRECTIONS: Choose the answer that means the same as the underlined word.

4. <u>Thrilling</u> ride

- (F) long
- (G) boring
- (H) exciting
- (J) interesting

5. <u>Dishonest</u> advertisement

- (A) trustworthy
- (B) imaginary
- (C) true
- (D) false

DIRECTIONS: Choose the answer that means the opposite of the underlined word.

6. He decided to <u>continue</u>.

- (F) stop
- (G) go on
- (H) roost
- (J) sleep

7. She was a <u>mighty</u> warrior.

- (A) great
- (B) strong
- (C) famous
- (D) weak

STOP

TAKS Reading—Objective 2

The student will apply knowledge of literary elements to understand culturally diverse written texts.

(3.11) Reading/text structures/literary concepts

The student analyzes the characteristics of various types of texts. The student is expected to

(H) analyze characters, including their traits, feelings, relationships, and changes (1–3); *(See pages 24–25.)*

(I) identify the importance of the setting to a story's meaning (1–3); and *(See pages 26–27.)*

(J) recognize the story problem(s) or plot (1–3). *(See pages 28–29.)*

Reading/Text Structures/Literary Concepts

Objective 2

Expectation: *analyze characters, including their traits, feelings, relationships, and changes*

From *Little Women* by Louisa May Alcott

Meg, the eldest of the four, was sixteen, and very pretty, being plump and fair, with large eyes, plenty of soft, brown hair, a sweet mouth, and white hands, of which she was rather vain. Fifteen-year-old Jo was very tall, thin, and reminded one of a colt . . . She had a decided mouth, a comical nose, and sharp, gray eyes, which appeared to see everything, and were by turns fierce, funny, or thoughtful. Her long, thick hair was her one beauty . . . Elizabeth—or Beth as everyone called her—was a rosy, smooth-haired, bright-eyed girl of thirteen, with a shy manner, a timid voice, and a peaceful expression, which was seldom disturbed. She seemed to live in a happy world of her own . . . . Amy, though the youngest, was a most important person—in her own opinion at least. A regular snow maiden, with blue eyes, and yellow hair curling on her shoulders; pale and slender, and always carrying herself like a young lady mindful of her manners.

GO

Reading/Text Structures/Literary Concepts

Objective 2

Expectation: *analyze characters, including their traits, feelings, relationships, and changes*

DIRECTIONS: Use the details from the paragraph to answer the questions.

1. Which of the characters is the oldest?
- (A) Amy
- (B) Beth
- (C) Meg
- (D) Jo

2. Which of the characters is the youngest?
- (F) Amy
- (G) Beth
- (H) Meg
- (J) Jo

3. Which of the characters is shy?
- (A) Amy
- (B) Beth
- (C) Meg
- (D) Jo

4. Which of the characters is tall?
- (F) Amy
- (G) Beth
- (H) Meg
- (J) Jo

5. Which of the characters thinks of herself as important?
- (A) Amy
- (B) Beth
- (C) Meg
- (D) Jo

6. Which of the characters is probably the smartest?
- (F) Amy
- (G) Beth
- (H) Meg
- (J) Jo

7. Which of the characters is probably the quietest?
- (A) Amy
- (B) Beth
- (C) Meg
- (D) Jo

8. Which of the characters is probably very polite?
- (F) Amy
- (G) Beth
- (H) Meg
- (J) Jo

9. Which of the characters takes pride in her hands?
- (A) Amy
- (B) Beth
- (C) Meg
- (D) Jo

STOP

Reading/Text Structures/Literary Concepts

Objective 2

Expectation: *identify the importance of the setting to a story's meaning*

Anna's Favorite Time

The wind blew softly, rippling the grasses across the prairie. Everywhere that Anna looked, she saw sky. She picked up the heavy iron pot and placed it back on the fire. As the sun began to set, she was glad for the shade of her sunbonnet. The sky lit up with pink, orange, and gold. Anna stirred the stew while she looked at the beauty all around her. She knew that Pa and the others would be hungry when they returned so she decided to prepare the meal. She climbed into the back of the covered wagon and searched through the food box for the tin plates and cups. Before the sun had slipped over the horizon, the stew was ready and everyone gathered around the fire for a warm meal. It was Anna's favorite time of day.

GO

Reading/Text Structures/Literary Concepts

Objective 2

Expectation: *identify the importance of the setting to a story's meaning*

DIRECTIONS: Choose the best answer.

1. This story most likely takes place in _____ .

- (A) a made-up time
- (B) the past
- (C) the present
- (D) the future

2. One clue that tells what time period in which the story takes place is _____ .

- (F) Anna is cooking in a heavy iron pot
- (G) Anna climbs into the back of a covered wagon
- (H) Anna decides to prepare a meal
- (J) everyone gathers around the fire

3. The setting of the story is _____ .

- (A) the prairie
- (B) the mountains
- (C) the city
- (D) the ocean

4. Which of the following would you be most likely to find in this setting?

- (F) tall buildings
- (G) a herd of buffaloes
- (H) boats
- (J) people skiing

5. This story takes place at what time of day?

- (A) early morning
- (B) lunchtime
- (C) afternoon
- (D) early evening

6. One clue that tells what time of day the story takes place is that _____ .

- (F) the wind blew softly
- (G) the sun began to set
- (H) Pa and the others would be hungry
- (J) it was Anna's favorite time of day

7. One detail that does not give a clue about what time period in which the story takes place is that _____ .

- (A) Anna wore a sunbonnet
- (B) the plates and cups were made of tin
- (C) they ate around the fire
- (D) none of these

STOP

Reading/Text Structures/Literary Concepts

Objective   ***Expectation:*** *recognize the story problem(s) or plot*
2

Bits's Bad Summer

Bits was a small, gray squirrel who lived in a big maple tree on Alten Road. She had a nice, dry nest in the tree. She had lots of trees around her where she could find nuts and seeds. There was a little stream for water. Bits had a happy life . . . until a new guest came to stay in the yellow house for the summer. This person had red hair and she owned a big, black cat. The cat spent all day, every day, outside.

Bits knew by instinct that the cat scared her, but she didn't know why. A cat bite, even a little nip, can kill a squirrel in a single day. Cats are fast and silent when they hunt. Even a cat that has been fed will hunt small animals. That's the cat's instinct.

Most of the people on Alten Road kept their cats indoors. But the guest at the yellow house let her cat out every morning. The cat created other dangers for Bits. Squirrels are usually careful when they cross streets, but not if a cat is chasing them. Bits had almost been hit by a truck one day when the black cat was chasing her.

Bits grew very hungry and thirsty. All of her food was buried in the ground. But the cat was looking for someone to hunt. So Bits could not dig up the food she had stored. She could not go to the stream for water. Bits needed to dig for the nuts and seeds she had buried, but with the cat outside all day, she couldn't. The cat went inside at night, and that is when Bits had to go back to her nest. Squirrels do this to keep away from other hunters, such as owls.

Sometimes Bits was able to race down her tree and find a nut before the cat saw her. Bits was scared. She knew she had to be careful all the time. Then one day, just as the leaves were falling from the big maple trees, Bits saw the red-haired woman carrying a basket to her car. The woman put the basket with her other bags into the car and drove away. Bits's bad summer was over. She had survived.

GO ⇨

Reading/Text Structures/Literary Concepts

Objective 2   *Expectation:* recognize the story problem(s) or plot

---

DIRECTIONS: Choose the best answer.

1. **What happened to upset Bits's happy life?**
   - (A) The new guest left her cat outside all day.
   - (B) The new guest left her cat outside at night.
   - (C) The new guest left her cat inside.
   - (D) The new guest carried her cat in a basket.

2. **Why was this a problem?**
   - (F) Cats steal nuts.
   - (G) Cats can kill squirrels.
   - (H) Cats chase owls.
   - (J) Cats go inside at night.

3. **Which of these would <u>not</u> have frightened Bits?**
   - (A) owls
   - (B) trucks
   - (C) water
   - (D) cats

4. **What caused Bits to be frightened of the cat?**
   - (F) scent
   - (G) noise
   - (H) rumor
   - (J) instinct

5. **Why did Bits want to leave her nest?**
   - (A) to get food and water
   - (B) to hide her food from the cat
   - (C) to warn other squirrels
   - (D) to get into the yellow house

6. **When did the cat leave?**
   - (F) after the first night
   - (G) in the fall
   - (H) never
   - (J) after about one year

7. **Why didn't Bits want to get her food at night?**
   - (A) She couldn't see as well.
   - (B) She was too tired.
   - (C) Other hunters were out.
   - (D) She couldn't find it.

8. **How was Bits's problem solved?**
   - (F) The cat went inside at night.
   - (G) Bits found a new nest.
   - (H) Sometimes Bits was able to race down her tree.
   - (J) The guest left at the end of summer.

STOP

Objective

2

Mini-Test

Skating

It was a sunny spring day and Jason couldn't wait for Tashara to show him how to use his new inline skates at the park. Jason had always wanted skates, and finally got them for his birthday. Now, he was ready for his first lesson.

Almost as soon as they got to the park, however, Michael raced by the slower skaters with a mocking sneer. "Show-off," Jason said.

Suddenly, Jason heard a loud crash on the other side of the park fence. "What was that?" asked Tashara.

From around the corner limped Michael, covered with twigs and leaves. "I don't think we have to worry about show-offs anymore," Jason said with a smile.

DIRECTIONS: Choose the best answer.

1. What is the setting for this story?

- (A) a parking lot
- (B) a park
- (C) a sporting goods store
- (D) Michael's house

2. This story is set in the _____.

- (F) past
- (G) future
- (H) present
- (J) none of these

3. Jason _____.

- (A) is friends with Tashara
- (B) is new to skating
- (C) just had a birthday
- (D) all of these

4. Tashara is _____.

- (F) a better skater than Jason
- (G) a better skater than Michael
- (H) not a skater
- (J) older than Jason

5. Michael is _____.

- (A) friendly
- (B) selfish
- (C) pleasant
- (D) a show-off

6. Jason and Michael _____.

- (F) are the same age
- (G) are both good skaters
- (H) are not friends
- (J) are brothers

TAKS Reading—Objective 3

The student will use a variety of strategies to analyze culturally diverse written texts.

(3.9) Reading/comprehension

The student uses a variety of strategies to comprehend selections read aloud and selections read independently. The student is expected to

(C) retell [or act out] the order of important events in stories (K–3); and *(See pages 32–33.)*

(I) represent text information in different ways, including story maps, graphs, and charts (2–3). *(See pages 34–35.)*

(3.11) Reading/text structures/literary concepts

The student analyzes the characteristics of various types of texts. The student is expected to

(A) distinguish different forms of texts, including lists, newsletters, and signs and the functions they serve (K–3); and *(See pages 36–37.)*

(C) recognize the distinguishing features of familiar genres, including stories, [poems], and informational texts (1–3). *(See pages 38–39.)*

Reading/Comprehension

Expectation: *retell [or act out] the order of important events in stories*

Marco Polo

It is difficult to imagine what the world was like in 1254. Europe was living in an age that we call the Medieval Period. It was a time of castles, knights and nobles, swords and lances, and many wars.

It was in that time that Marco Polo was born in Venice, Italy. Life in Venice was different from life in most of Europe. Venice was a city of beautiful buildings and water canals. Many merchants brought riches from other countries to trade in Venice. Marco Polo's father and uncle were merchants. They had traveled to a far-off country called Cathay. (Cathay is now called China.) There they had become friends with the great ruler, Kublai Khan. He invited them to return.

When Marco Polo was seventeen years old, he began a journey to China with his father and uncle. They sailed the Indian Ocean and crossed the deserts and mountains of Asia on camels. The journey to China took three years.

Kublai Khan greeted the Polos and showered them with gifts. He was especially impressed with Marco, who could speak four languages.

Khan sent Marco on many trips through China. On these trips, Marco saw many amazing things that he had never seen in Europe, such as coal used as fuel, paper money instead of coins, and papermaking and printing processes. Marco made many notes about life in China.

After almost twenty years in China, the Polos began their journey home to Italy. Kublai Khan gave them many gifts of ivory, silk, jewels, and jade.

When they returned to Venice, they found their city at war. Marco Polo was put in prison. He spent his time writing a book about his years in China. The book is called *Descriptions of the World*. It became the most popular book in Europe. Because of the book, many people in Europe learned about life in China.

GO →

Reading/Comprehension

Objective 3

Expectation: *retell [or act out] the order of important events in stories*

DIRECTIONS: Choose the best answer.

1. **Which sentence best states the main idea of this passage?**
   - (A) Travel to China took a long time in 1254.
   - (B) Kublai Khan welcomed the Polos when they arrived.
   - (C) Marco Polo could speak four languages.
   - (D) Marco Polo became famous for writing about his travels in China.

2. **Which event happened first?**
   - (F) Marco Polo spent 20 years in China.
   - (G) Marco Polo's father and uncle became friends with Kublai Khan.
   - (H) Khan sent Marco on many trips through China.
   - (J) Khan was very impressed with Marco Polo.

3. **Which of these had Marco never seen before?**
   - (A) people riding camels
   - (B) coal used as fuel
   - (C) large ships that crossed the ocean
   - (D) water canals through cities

4. **Marco Polo's father and uncle were _____ .**
   - (F) geographers
   - (G) historians
   - (H) warriors
   - (J) merchants

5. **Which of the following is not true? When Marco Polo returned to Venice _____ .**
   - (A) he became a rich merchant
   - (B) the city was at war
   - (C) he was put in prison
   - (D) he wrote a book

6. **How old was Marco Polo when he wrote his book?**
   - (F) in his 60s
   - (G) in his 30s
   - (H) in his 40s
   - (J) in his 20s

7. **Cathay is now known as _____ .**
   - (A) Korea
   - (B) Hawaii
   - (C) Indonesia
   - (D) China

8. **Kublai Khan was impressed with Marco Polo because he _____ .**
   - (F) sailed the ship from Venice
   - (G) had written *Descriptions of the World*
   - (H) spoke four languages
   - (J) explained papermaking

STOP

Reading/Comprehension

Objective 3

Expectation: *represent text information in different ways, including story maps, graphs, and charts*

Symphony Instruments

Emmeline is going with her father to hear the symphony orchestra. She likes listening to the violins. Her father likes listening to the woodwinds and brass. When she arrives, her father explains that the orchestra musicians must be seated in special places in order to make the music sound just right. The diagram below shows where musicians normally sit in an orchestra.

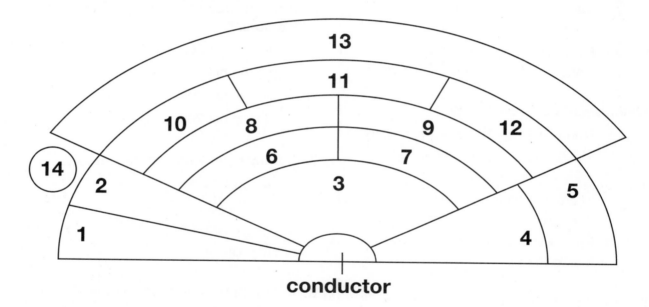

conductor

Strings

1. First Violins

2. Second Violins

3. Violas

4. Cellos

5. Double Basses

Woodwinds

6. Flutes

7. Oboes

8. Clarinets

9. Bassoons

Brass

10. Horns

11. Trumpets

12. Trombones/Tuba

13. Percussion/Timpani

14. Harp

GO

Name _____ Date _____

Reading/Comprehension

Objective 3

Expectation: represent text information in different ways, including story maps, graphs, and charts

DIRECTIONS: Use the diagram on the previous page to answer the questions.

1. **How many types of instruments are in the string section?**
   - (A) 5
   - (B) 4
   - (C) 6
   - (D) 14

2. **Oboes are in the _____ section.**
   - (F) woodwinds
   - (G) brass
   - (H) strings
   - (J) percussion

3. **Bassoons are in the _____ section.**
   - (A) percussion
   - (B) woodwinds
   - (C) strings
   - (D) brass

4. **Number 6 in the diagram stands for _____ .**
   - (F) bassoons
   - (G) flutes
   - (H) percussion/timpani
   - (J) trombones/tuba

5. **The harp is behind the _____ .**
   - (A) trumpets
   - (B) cellos
   - (C) second violins
   - (D) flutes

6. **The conductor stands directly in front of the _____ .**
   - (F) harp
   - (G) violas
   - (H) double basses
   - (J) horns

STOP

Reading/Text Structures/Literary Concepts

Objective 3

Expectation: distinguish different forms of texts, including lists, newsletters, and signs and the functions they serve

DIRECTIONS: Read the passage and answer the questions that follow.

Tornado Strikes Kansas

April 2, 2003 — Yesterday, at exactly 3:38 P.M., a large tornado touched down on a farm near Topeka. No injuries were reported. However, many crops were destroyed by the high winds.

1. Where would you most likely find this information?

- Ⓐ in an advertisement
- Ⓑ on a sign
- Ⓒ in a newspaper
- Ⓓ in an encyclopedia

2. What is the headline of this story?

- Ⓕ April 2, 2003
- Ⓖ Tornado Strikes Kansas
- Ⓗ 3:38 P.M.
- Ⓙ Topeka

DIRECTIONS: Choose the best answer.

3. Which of these would most likely be found in a mystery story?

- Ⓐ The President lives in Washington, D.C.
- Ⓑ Bears eat many different foods.
- Ⓒ Dolores opened the door slowly, but no one was there.
- Ⓓ Before you can fix a leaky roof, you must find the leak.

4. The purpose of a glossary in a book is to _____ .

- Ⓕ give definitions of important words
- Ⓖ give the name of the author and publisher
- Ⓗ give the titles of the chapters of the book
- Ⓙ give the page numbers of specific items

5. The purpose of a table of contents in a book is to _____ .

- Ⓐ give definitions of important words
- Ⓑ give the name of the author and publisher
- Ⓒ give the titles of the chapters of the book
- Ⓓ give the page number of specific items

6. The purpose of an index in a book is to _____ .

- Ⓕ give definitions of important words
- Ⓖ give the name of the author and publisher
- Ⓗ give the titles of the chapters of the book
- Ⓙ give the page numbers of specific items

GO

Reading/Text Structures/Literary Concepts

Objective 3   *Expectation:* distinguish different forms of texts, including lists, newsletters, and signs and the functions they serve

---

DIRECTIONS: Read numbers 7 through 17. Then choose where this information is most likely to be found.

    A. in an atlas
    B. in a dictionary
    C. in an encyclopedia
    D. in a newspaper

7. _____   **pronunciation of a word**

8. _____   **types of animals in a rain forest**

9. _____   **map of Pennsylvania**

10. _____   **comic strip**

11. _____   **place where Abraham Lincoln was born**

12. _____   **report of a fire in your neighborhood**

13. _____   **definition of the word** *concave*

14. _____   **latitude and longitude of Paris, France**

15. _____   **job listings**

16. _____   **the date that World War II ended**

17. _____   **how to break a word into syllables**

DIRECTIONS: Choose the best answer.

What I remember most about that big old house in Iowa was the kitchen, a room that was always warm and always smelled wonderful.

18. **This sentence would most likely be found in _____ .**
    Ⓐ a newspaper article
    Ⓑ an autobiography
    Ⓒ a fairy tale
    Ⓓ a science book

19. **Which of these would most likely be found in a newspaper article?**
    Ⓕ "Now hold on there," said the sheriff, "we don't put up with things like that in this town."
    Ⓖ It wasn't a star they were looking at, but a spaceship, and it was coming right at them.
    Ⓗ Guido said good-bye to his family, picked up his bags, and joined the crowd walking toward the ship.
    Ⓙ A recent report from the school board stated that there are more students in our school than there were last year.

STOP

Reading/Text Structures/Literary Concepts

Objective 3   *Expectation: recognize the distinguishing features of familiar genres, including stories, [poems], and informational texts*

DIRECTIONS: Read the following passages and answer the questions that follow.

My Backpack

My backpack's so heavy   My breath is so short
It must weigh a ton.   I need oxygen.
With thousands of books —   When I stoop over,
My work's never done.   It makes me fall down.
My arms are so sore   I think I'll just stay here
I can't lift a pen.   All squashed on the ground.

1. This passage is which genre (type) of literature?

(A) poetry

(B) fiction

(C) biography

(D) fable

2. What clues helped you decide what genre it is?

(F) It has a moral at the end.

(G) It is about something real.

(H) It has rhyming words.

(J) It gives details about a real person's life.

The Ant and the Dove

An Ant went to the bank of a stream to get a drink of water. The stream was so fast that it carried the Ant away. Just as the Ant was about to drown, a Dove sitting on a tree overhanging the water plucked a leaf and let it fall into the stream close to the Ant. The Ant climbed onto the leaf and floated safely to dry land. Shortly afterwards, a hunter came and stood under the tree and set a trap for the Dove. When the Ant saw what was happening, he quickly stung the hunter. In pain, the hunter yelled and threw down the trap. The Dove heard the noise and flew away to safety. The moral of the story is: One good turn deserves another.

3. This passage is which genre (type) of literature?

(A) poetry

(B) fiction

(C) biography

(D) fable

4. What clues helped you decide?

(F) It has a moral at the end.

(G) It is about something real.

(H) It has rhyming words.

(J) It gives details about a real person's life.

Reading/Text Structures/Literary Concepts

Objective 3

Expectation: recognize the distinguishing features of familiar genres, including stories, [poems], and informational texts

---

John Glenn

On November 5,1998, Senator John Glenn traveled into space as the oldest astronaut ever. He was 77 years old.

This was not the first time John Glenn was in space. In 1962, when he was 40 years old, John Glenn was the first American to circle Earth in orbit. He traveled on the *Friendship 7*. Scientists wanted to observe Glenn's reaction to the space environment.

In 1998, John Glenn went into space on the space shuttle *Discovery*. This time, scientists wanted to observe the reaction of an older man in the space environment.

Glenn was an American hero both times he traveled into space.

---

5. This passage is which genre (type) of literature?

- (A) poetry
- (B) fiction
- (C) biography
- (D) fable

6. What clues helped you decide what genre it is?

- (F) It has a moral at the end.
- (G) It is about something real.
- (H) It has rhyming words.
- (J) It gives details about a real person's life.

STOP

Objective

3

| Mini-Test |

Below is a list that Danny made to help him remember the things he needs to do.

Things To Do Today

___X___ Make bed

___X___ Brush teeth

___X___ Take science project to school

_____ Return library books before lunch

_____ Take home math book

_____ Go to Ramon's birthday party after school

DIRECTIONS: Choose the best answer using information from Danny's list.

1. The purpose of Danny's list is _____ .

(A) to help him remember the things he needs to do

(B) to remind him to finish his science project

(C) to show his dentist his good habits

(D) to show his parents he has earned his allowance

2. What is the first thing Danny did today?

(F) return his library books

(G) brush his teeth

(H) make his bed

(J) go to Ramon's birthday party

3. What is the next thing Danny needs to do?

(A) take home his math book

(B) go to Ramon's birthday party

(C) return his library books

(D) make his bed

4. Danny has checked off a few things on his list. What time of day is it now?

(F) first thing in the morning

(G) sometime before lunch

(H) sometime after lunch

(J) after school

DIRECTIONS: Read the passage and answer the question.

Votes for Women

Elizabeth Cady Stanton was born in 1815. Her parents were important people and gave their daughter a complete education. She married antislavery speaker Henry Stanton in 1840.

Along with Lucretia Mot, Stanton helped to organize the 1848 Women's Rights Convention at Seneca Falls, New York. She became friends with Susan B. Anthony soon after this, and the two remained friends throughout their lives. Stanton became a popular speaker throughout the United States after the Civil War. She spoke about social reform issues.

After devoting most of her life to fighting for women's suffrage, Stanton died 18 years before the passage of the Nineteenth Amendment. This amendment finally gave women the right to vote.

5. This passage is which genre (type) of literature?

(A) poetry

(B) fiction

(C) biography

(D) fable

STOP

TAKS Reading—Objective 4

The student will apply critical-thinking skills to analyze culturally diverse written texts.

(3.9) Reading/comprehension
The student uses a variety of strategies to comprehend selections read aloud and selections read independently. The student is expected to
- **(F)** make and explain inferences from texts such as determining important ideas, causes and effects, making predictions, and drawing conclusions (1–3); and *(See pages 42–43.)*
- **(J)** distinguish fact from opinion in various texts, including news stories and advertisements (3). *(See pages 44–45.)*

(3.10) Reading/literary response
The student responds to various texts. The student is expected to
- **(C)** support interpretations or conclusions with examples drawn from text (2–3). *(See pages 46–47.)*

Reading/Comprehension

Objective 4

Expectation: make and explain inferences from texts such as determining important ideas, causes and effects, making predictions, and drawing conclusions

On Stage

MR. BOUIE: (shaking his finger at Art) How many times do I have to tell you to quit doing that?

ART: I can't help it! If I could lock them in a closet and leave them there, I could stop.

MR. BOUIE: Well, that would be odd. If you don't quit soon your poor fingernails are going to forget how to grow!

ART: Hey, come on, Dad. I bet you did it when you were a kid.

MR. BOUIE: Never did.

ART: By the way, when can we visit Sizzle?

MR. BOUIE: Sizzle may not even recognize us.

ART: (very surprised) She'd never forget me!

MR. BOUIE: She may not want a visit. You know she'll look different now.

ART: I know she's expecting. (getting excited) Do you think she'll have more than one?

MR. BOUIE: (sitting down on the living room couch) Probably not. They usually have one at a time.

ART: I can't wait to see it! (walking behind the couch so his dad can't see him) Poor Sizzle. She hated it when we took her to the zoo.

MR. BOUIE: Yes, but later she only seemed to notice us when we brought her bananas.

ART: I don't blame her; we abandoned her! It was Uncle Jack's fault. (biting his nails, but walking in front of the couch) I wanted to keep her!

MR. BOUIE: Now don't blame Jack. You were delighted when he brought her home. (sees Art biting nails) Art! (shouting) How many times do I have to tell you to stop doing that?

GO

Reading/Comprehension

Objective 4

Expectation: make and explain inferences from texts such as determining important ideas, causes and effects, making predictions, and drawing conclusions

---

DIRECTIONS: Answer the following questions based on your reading of the play.

1. **What is the relationship between Mr. Bouie and Art?**
   - (A) brothers
   - (B) father and son
   - (C) uncle and nephew
   - (D) teacher and student

2. **What is the relationship between Art and Jack?**
   - (F) brothers
   - (G) father and son
   - (H) uncle and nephew
   - (J) teacher and student

3. **What does Art wish he could put away in a closet?**
   - (A) his coat
   - (B) his fingernails
   - (C) his boots
   - (D) the couch

4. **Who is Sizzle?**
   - (F) a bird
   - (G) a dog
   - (H) a monkey
   - (J) an elephant

5. **Where is she now?**
   - (A) the zoo
   - (B) Africa
   - (C) the pet store
   - (D) the back yard

6. **How has she changed?**
   - (F) She now hates bananas.
   - (G) She has grown taller.
   - (H) She has learned sign language.
   - (J) She is expecting a baby.

7. **What might make Sizzle notice Art?**
   - (A) Uncle Jack
   - (B) a banana
   - (C) a whistle
   - (D) a round of applause

8. **How did Sizzle get to Art's house?**
   - (F) She ran away from the circus.
   - (G) He bought her from a pet shop.
   - (H) Uncle Jack bought her.
   - (J) He was watching her for a friend.

STOP

Reading/Comprehension

Objective 4

Expectation: distinguish fact from opinion in various texts, including news stories and advertisements

The Loch Ness Monster

Do you know about one of the most famous monsters in the world? The Loch Ness monster is a large animal that some people believe lives in Loch Ness, a deep dark lake in Scotland.

For many years, hundreds of people have reported seeing something strange in the lake. They have even given it the nickname "Nessie." Nessie is said to be about 30 feet long, with a long, slender neck, one or two humps, and flippers. Some witnesses say it looks like the drawings of what a plesiosaur must have looked like. The plesiosaur was a reptile that lived 65 million years ago during the time

of the dinosaurs and is thought to be extinct. In addition to the eyewitness reports, there are even pictures that have been taken of a large animal-like shape in the water.

In 1987, Operation Deep Scan went to Loch Ness. This group of researchers used 20 boats to sweep the entire loch with sonar. Sonar is a kind of technology that uses sound waves to detect things under water. During this operation, they found three large things that could not be explained. Two later groups also found mysterious underwater things. One was a moving target the size of a small whale. Scientists are still trying to solve the mystery of Nessie.

GO

Reading/Comprehension

Objective 4

Expectation: *distinguish fact from opinion in various texts, including news stories and advertisements*

DIRECTIONS: Choose the best answer.

1. **Which of the following is a fact about Nessie?**

   (A) Nessie is a dinosaur.

   (B) Nessie has a long, slender neck.

   (C) Nessie has flippers.

   (D) Nessie is a mystery.

2. **Which of the following statements about the Loch Ness monster cannot be proven?**

   (F) There is a real place in Scotland called Loch Ness.

   (G) Nessie prefers to swim in the deepest part of the lake.

   (H) People have taken pictures of something in Loch Ness.

   (J) There are people who believe that Nessie exists.

3. **Which of the following is an opinion?**

   (A) People have given the monster the nickname "Nessie."

   (B) People have taken pictures of something in Loch Ness.

   (C) People who believe in the Loch Ness monster are wrong.

   (D) People have used sonar to find Nessie.

4. **If you were writing a factual report about the Loch Ness monster, which of the following sentences would you not include?**

   (F) The Loch Ness Monster has a long slender neck and flippers.

   (G) Many people believe that a monster lives in a deep lake in Scotland.

   (H) Scientists are still trying to solve the mystery of what is in Loch Ness.

   (J) The Loch Ness monster is one of the world's famous mysteries.

5. **What was found after the loch was searched with sonar?**

   (A) a sunken ship

   (B) huge rocks

   (C) three large things that could not be explained

   (D) a pod of whales

STOP

45

Name _____ Date _____

Reading/Literary Response

Objective 4

Expectation: *support interpretations or conclusions with examples drawn from text*

DIRECTIONS: Read the passage and answer the questions.

Traveling Seeds

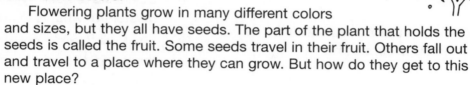

Everyone knows that flowering plants cannot fly, run, or walk. But, through their seeds, they can move from place to place. That is why you see new plants growing each year where there were none before.

Flowering plants grow in many different colors and sizes, but they all have seeds. The part of the plant that holds the seeds is called the fruit. Some seeds travel in their fruit. Others fall out and travel to a place where they can grow. But how do they get to this new place?

Some seeds stick to people's clothes or animals' fur and are carried from place to place. The seeds drop off and form new plants where they fall. Other seeds may be scattered by wind and rain.

However it happens, seeds certainly move.

1. **From the passage you can conclude that _____ .**
   - (A) seeds move in many ways
   - (B) seeds grow from wind and rain
   - (C) seeds do not move
   - (D) seeds and fruit are good snacks

2. **Based on the passage, why do you see new plants growing in places there were none the year before?**
   - (F) Seeds must grow near the plant that grew them.
   - (G) Through their seeds, plants move from place to place.
   - (H) Flowering plants grow in many different colors.
   - (J) People buy seeds and plant them.

3. **From the passage you can conclude that _____ .**
   - (A) seeds may arrive in the mail
   - (B) your dog may carry seeds to a new place
   - (C) a storm would not carry seeds to a new place
   - (D) plants will not grow where there were none before

4. **Which of the following is not a way that seeds travel to a new place?**
   - (F) on your shirt
   - (G) in the wind
   - (H) on a walking plant
   - (J) on an animal's fur

Reading/Literary Response

Objective 4

Expectation: *support interpretations or conclusions with examples drawn from text*

DIRECTIONS: Read the passage and answer the questions.

Glue

Glue is an adhesive. It is used to stick things together. There are three basic kinds of glue: hide glue, bone glue, and fish glue. Glues are made of gelatin, which comes from boiling animal parts and bones.

Long ago, people used other materials as glue. Ancient people used sticky juices from plants and insects. This was mixed with vegetable coloring and used as paint on rocks and caves. Egyptians learned to boil animal hides and bones to make glue. This was much like the glue that is used today.

Today, there are many special kinds of glue. Epoxy glue is made to stick in high temperatures, even if it becomes wet. "Super" glue is the strongest of glues. It can stick even with two tons of pressure against it.

5. What are the three basic kinds of glue?

- (A) paper, wood, plastic
- (B) white, paste, stick
- (C) fabric, metal, wall
- (D) hide, bone, fish

6. From the passage you can conclude that _____ .

- (F) glue is a modern invention
- (G) glue cannot stick in extreme heat
- (H) people have glued things together for thousands of years
- (J) paint was sometimes used as glue

7. Which of the following phrases gives the best definition for glue?

- (A) useful for repairs or art activities
- (B) an adhesive used to stick things together
- (C) something that sticks in high temperatures
- (D) mixture of vegetable coloring and bones

STOP

Name _____   Date _____

DIRECTIONS: Read the article and complete the questions.

A Brief History of Chocolate

Today, everyone loves chocolate, but before the 1900s, most Americans had never tasted it. In ancient times, as early as 1000 B.C., people enjoyed chocolate in a drink. It was made from cocoa beans and bitter spices. Later, people learned to add sugar to make the drink sweeter.

In 1828, a Dutch chemist found a way to make the fine powder we know as cocoa. Soon, candy makers began to find ways to make candy from cocoa.

In 1875, Daniel Peter and Henri Nestlé found a way to produce milk chocolate. Making milk chocolate took a lot of work and was very expensive. It also took a lot of time, but it was worth every minute.

In the early 1900s, Milton Hershey found a way to mass produce milk chocolate, or make large amounts of it, in his factory in Hershey, Pennsylvania. This took less time and work than the old process, so it was not as expensive to make milk chocolate. Hershey sold his chocolate bars for five cents each. This was the first time most people could afford to eat and enjoy chocolate.

1. **Why do you think that most children did not get to eat milk chocolate before the early 1900s?**

   (A) It was too expensive.

   (B) It was made from bitter spices.

   (C) It was bad for their teeth.

   (D) It was only available in a drink.

2. **The milk chocolate made by Milton Hershey was _____ .**

   (F) bitter

   (G) hard to mass produce

   (H) delicious

   (J) expensive

3. **Which of the following is a fact from the article?**

   (A) Today, everyone loves chocolate.

   (B) In 1875, Daniel Peter and Henri Nestlé found a way to produce milk chocolate.

   (C) A French chemist found a way to make the fine powder we know as cocoa.

   (D) Making milk chocolate was quick and easy.

4. **Which of the following is an opinion?**

   (F) Daniel Peter and Henri Nestlé found a way to produce milk chocolate.

   (G) As early as 1000 B.C., people enjoyed chocolate in a drink.

   (H) Today, everyone loves chocolate.

   (J) Milton Hershey found a way to mass produce milk chocolate in his factory in Hershey, Pennsylvania.

5. **Which of the following contains both a fact and an opinion?**

   (A) Candy makers began to find ways to make candy from cocoa.

   (B) In the early 1900s, Milton Hershey found a way to mass produce milk chocolate.

   (C) Making milk chocolate took a lot of work and was very expensive.

   (D) It also took a lot of time, but it was worth every minute.

How Am I Doing?

Objective 1 Mini-Test Page 22 **Number Correct**	**7** answers correct	**Great Job!** Move on to the section test on page 51.
	5–6 answers correct	**You're almost there!** But you still need a little practice. Review practice pages 8–21 before moving on to the section test on page 51.
	0–4 answers correct	**Oops!** Time to review what you have learned and try again. Review the practice section on pages 8–21. Then retake the test on page 22. Now move on to the section test on page 51.
Objective 2 Mini-Test Page 30 **Number Correct**	**6** answers correct	**Awesome!** Move on to the section test on page 51.
	4–5 answers correct	**You're almost there!** But you still need a little practice. Review practice pages 24–29 before moving on to the section test on page 51.
	0–3 answers correct	**Oops!** Time to review what you have learned and try again. Review the practice section on pages 24–29. Then retake the test on page 30. Now move on to the section test on page 51.

How Am I Doing?

Objective 3 Mini-Test Page 40 **Number Correct**	**5** answers correct	**Great Job!** Move on to the section test on page 51.
	3–4 answers correct	**You're almost there!** But you still need a little practice. Review practice pages 32–39 before moving on to the section test on page 51.
	0–2 answers correct	**Oops!** Time to review what you have learned and try again. Review the practice section on pages 32–39. Then retake the test on page 40. Now move on to the section test on page 51.
Objective 4 Mini-Test Page 48 **Number Correct**	**5** answers correct	**Awesome!** Move on to the section test on page 51.
	3–4 answers correct	**You're almost there!** But you still need a little practice. Review practice pages 42–47 before moving on to the section test on page 51.
	0–2 answers correct	**Oops!** Time to review what you have learned and try again. Review the practice section on pages 42–47. Then retake the test on page 48. Now move on to the section test on page 51.

Final Test for
Reading
for pages 8–48

DIRECTIONS: Choose the best answer.

1. **Find the answer that means the same or about the same as the underlined word.**
   long <u>journey</u>
   - (A) story
   - (B) movie
   - (C) road
   - (D) trip

2. **Find the word that means the opposite of the underlined word.**
   <u>thrilling</u> ride
   - (F) long
   - (G) exciting
   - (H) boring
   - (J) interesting

3. **Read the sentence with the missing word and then read the question. Find the best answer to the question.**

   The weather will _____ tomorrow.
   Which word means the weather will get better?
   - (A) improve
   - (B) change
   - (C) worsen
   - (D) vary

4. **Find the word that fits best in the blank.**
   Dogs need _____ to stay healthy.
   - (F) treats
   - (G) dishes
   - (H) exercise
   - (J) collars

5. **Choose the word that correctly completes both sentences.**
   Who will _____ this problem?
   The _____ on the shovel is broken.
   - (A) solve
   - (B) blade
   - (C) cause
   - (D) handle

6. **Which word could be a heading for the other three words?**
   - (F) fly
   - (G) insect
   - (H) ant
   - (J) beetle

7. **Which word in this sentence has a prefix?**
   The largest bottle of ketchup was unopened.
   - (A) largest
   - (B) bottle
   - (C) ketchup
   - (D) unopened

8. **Which word in this sentence has a suffix?**
   Alisha was late and quietly left the party.
   - (F) late
   - (G) quietly
   - (H) left
   - (J) party

GO

9. **Read the definitions in this dictionary entry. Which definition best fits the word *express* as it is used in the sentence below?**

The express will get us home quickly.

ex · press [ik spres´] v. **1.** to put into words **2.** to show or reveal **3.** to send quickly *adj.* **4.** clear or easily understood **5.** quick *n.* **6.** a direct train

- (A) 1
- (B) 2
- (C) 5
- (D) 6

10. **Sally is reading a book called *Home Gardening for Young People*. Which of these sentences would most likely be at the beginning of the book?**

- (F) After you have planted the seeds, you'll have to keep them watered so they don't dry out.
- (G) Few things are as rewarding as tending a garden.
- (H) Now comes the fun part, eating vegetables you have raised.
- (J) The most difficult part of having a garden is making sure that weeds don't take over.

11. **Which sentence is most likely to come next in the story below?**

The travelers found themselves in a forest of talking trees. Just then, all the trees began talking at once. They were so loud that it was impossible to understand what they were saying.

- (A) Once upon a time, a group of travelers started on a long journey.
- (B) No one knew where they were and they became frightened.
- (C) Suddenly, the biggest tree said, "Quiet, everyone!"
- (D) The outside of the trunk of a tree is called the bark.

DIRECTIONS: Read the passage, then choose the best answer for each question.

Wendy Lost and Found

Wendy was scared. For the second time in her young life, she was lost. When the branch fell on her small house and the fence, she had barely escaped. She leaped across the fallen fence into the woods. Now the rain poured down and the wind howled. The little woodchuck shivered under a big oak tree. She did not know what to do.

When Wendy was a baby, her mother had died. She had been alone in the woods then, too. She could not find enough food. Then she hurt her paw. All day she scratched at a small hole in the ground, trying to make a burrow. Every night, she was hungry.

One day, Rita had found her. Rita had knelt down by Wendy's shallow burrow and set down an apple. Wendy limped slowly out and took the apple. It was the best thing she had ever tasted. Rita took the baby woodchuck to the wildlife center, and Wendy had lived there ever since. Most of the animals at the center were orphans. Rita taught them how to live in the wild, and then let them go when they were ready. But Wendy's paw did not heal well, and Rita knew that Wendy would never be able to go back to the wild. So Rita had made Wendy a house and a pen. Wendy even had a job—she visited schools with Rita so that students could learn all about woodchucks.

Now the storm had ruined Wendy's house. She did not know how to find Rita. At dawn, the rain ended. Wendy limped down to a big stream and sniffed the air. Maybe the center was across the stream. Wendy jumped onto a rock and then hopped to another one. She landed on her bad paw and fell into the fast-moving water. The little woodchuck struggled to keep her nose above water. The current tossed her against a tangle of branches. Wendy held on with all her might.

"There she is!" Wendy heard Rita's voice. Rita and Ben, another worker from the wildlife center, were across the stream. Rita waded out to the branches, lifted Wendy up, and wrapped her in a blanket. Wendy purred her thanks. By the time Ben and Rita got into the van to go back to the center, Wendy was fast asleep.

GO

12. What genre of literature is this passage?

(F) fable

(G) biography

(H) fiction

(J) poetry

13. This passage is mostly about _____ .

(A) a wildlife center worker

(B) a woodchuck who lives at a wildlife center

(C) a woodchuck who can do tricks

(D) a woodchuck who learns how to swim

14. How does the passage start?

(F) with Wendy's life as a baby

(G) in the middle of the storm

(H) with Wendy's visit to school

(J) when Wendy is in the stream

15. Why do you think the author wrote about Wendy's life as a baby?

(A) so the reader knows that Wendy has been lost before and knows what to do

(B) so the reader knows that Wendy can't live in the wild and is in danger

(C) so the reader knows that Wendy trusts people and will be all right

(D) so the reader knows that Wendy can find apples to eat

16. Which answer is a fact about woodchucks from the passage?

(F) Wendy loves apples.

(G) Woodchucks dig burrows.

(H) Woodchucks can climb tall fences.

(J) Wendy limps because of her hurt paw.

17. What is Rita's job?

(A) saving woodchucks from streams

(B) teaching science at a school

(C) gathering apples

(D) working at the wildlife center with animals

18. What are the settings for this passage?

(F) the woods and the wildlife center

(G) the school and the stream

(H) the school and the woods

(J) the wildlife center and Rita's house

19. Which of the following best summarizes the passage?

(A) Wendy is a woodchuck with a job— she visits schools with Rita so that students can learn about woodchucks.

(B) Wendy is an orphaned woodchuck who lives at the wildlife center. One night a storm destroyed her pen and she got lost in the woods. Rita saved her a second time.

(C) When Wendy the woodchuck was a baby she was lost in the woods. Then, Rita found her and took her to the wildlife center to live.

D   A storm destroyed Wendy the woodchuck's pen. She was so scared she ran into the woods and was lost for a second time.

20. What is the climax of the passage?

(F) when Wendy's mother dies

(G) when Rita gives Wendy an apple

(H) when Wendy falls into the stream

(J) when Rita wraps Wendy in a blanket

21. Why can't Wendy return to live in the wild?

(A) because she is an orphan

(B) because she has a job

(C) because her paw did not heal well

(D) because she can't swim

22. What event happened after Wendy jumped from rock to rock?

(F) She fell into the water.

(G) Her pen was destroyed by the storm.

(H) Rita gave her an apple.

(J) She leaped across the fence into the woods.

23. How do you think Wendy feels about Rita?

(A) She dislikes her.

(B) She is afraid of her.

(C) She doesn't know her.

(D) She trusts her.

24. What event from the passage supports the idea that Rita cares about Wendy?

(F) She jumps into the water to save Wendy.

(G) She brings Ben to look for Wendy.

(H) She takes Rita to schools.

(J) She falls asleep.

BACK TO SCHOOL SPECIAL

BUY A PAIR OF SHOES. GET TWO PAIRS OF SOCKS FOR FREE!

This special is good at our downtown store only, not at our Lakeview store.

This sales special is good from August 1–August 15 only.

If you buy a pair of shoes that costs at least $20.00, we'll give you two pairs of socks for FREE!*

*You must choose socks that cost less than $2.00 per pair

If you come into the store on the first day of the special, we'll give you a COUPON for an extra 10% off of your total purchase.

DIRECTIONS: Jessalyn, Juanita, and Daniel all read the sign above in the window of a shoe store. Answer these questions about the sign.

25. If Jessalyn went to the downtown store on August 1, she would _____ .

(A) get a coupon for an extra 10% off

(B) get one free pairs of socks

(C) buy a pair of $10.00 shoes

(D) be too late for the special

26. If Daniel bought a pair of $15.00 shoes on August 3, he would _____ .

(F) not get free socks

(G) get free socks

(H) be too early for the special

(J) be too late for the sale

Reading Test
Answer Sheet

1 (A) (B) (C) (D)
2 (F) (G) (H) (J)
3 (A) (B) (C) (D)
4 (F) (G) (H) (J)
5 (A) (B) (C) (D)
6 (F) (G) (H) (J)
7 (A) (B) (C) (D)
8 (F) (G) (H) (J)
9 (A) (B) (C) (D)
10 (F) (G) (H) (J)

11 (A) (B) (C) (D)
12 (F) (G) (H) (J)
13 (A) (B) (C) (D)
14 (F) (G) (H) (J)
15 (A) (B) (C) (D)
16 (F) (G) (H) (J)
17 (A) (B) (C) (D)
18 (F) (G) (H) (J)
19 (A) (B) (C) (D)
20 (F) (G) (H) (J)

21 (A) (B) (C) (D)
22 (F) (G) (H) (J)
23 (A) (B) (C) (D)
24 (F) (G) (H) (J)
25 (A) (B) (C) (D)
26 (F) (G) (H) (J)

Mathematics
Content Standards

The mathematics section of the state test measures knowledge in six different areas.

1) Objective 1: Number, operation, and quantitative reasoning

2) Objective 2: Patterns, relationships, and algebraic thinking

3) Objective 3: Geometry and spatial reasoning

4) Objective 4: Measurement

5) Objective 5: Probability and statistics

6) Objective 6: Underlying processes and mathematical tools

Mathematics
Table of Contents

Mathematics Chart
Grade 3

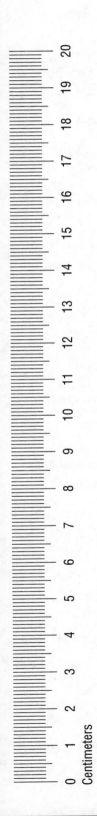

Length

Metric

1 meter = 100 centimeters

1 centimeter = 10 millimeters

Customary

1 yard = 3 feet

1 foot = 12 inches

Time

1 year = 365 days

1 year = 12 months

1 year = 52 weeks

1 week = 7 days

1 day = 24 hours

1 hour = 60 minutes

1 minute = 60 seconds

TAKS Mathematics—Objective 1

The student will demonstrate an understanding of numbers, operations, and quantitative reasoning.

(3.1) Number, operation, and quantitative reasoning

The student uses place value to communicate about increasingly large whole numbers in verbal and written form, including money. The student is expected to

- **(A)** use place value to read, write (in symbols and words), and describe the value of whole numbers through 999,999; *(See pages 59–60.)*
- **(B)** use place value to compare and order whole numbers through 9,999; and *(See pages 61–62.)*
- **(C)** determine the value of a collection of coins and bills. *(See pages 63–64.)*

(3.2) Number, operation, and quantitative reasoning

The student uses fraction names and symbols to describe fractional parts of whole objects or sets of objects. The student is expected to

- **(B)** compare fractional parts of whole objects or sets of objects in a problem situation using [concrete] models; and *(See pages 65–66.)*
- **(C)** use fraction names and symbols to describe fractional parts of whole objects or sets of objects with denominators of 12 or less. *(See pages 67–68.)*

(3.3) Number, operation, and quantitative reasoning

The student adds and subtracts to solve meaningful problems involving whole numbers. The student is expected to

- **(A)** model addition and subtraction using pictures, words, and numbers; and *(See pages 69–70.)*
- **(B)** select addition or subtraction and use the operation to solve problems involving whole numbers through 999. *(See pages 71–72.)*

(3.4) Number, operation, and quantitative reasoning

The student recognizes and solves problems in multiplication and division situations. The student is expected to

- **(B)** solve and record multiplication problems (one-digit multiplier); and *(See pages 73–74.)*
- **(C)** use models to solve division problems and use number sentences to record the solutions. *(See pages 75–76.)*

(3.5) Number, operation, and quantitative reasoning.

The student estimates to determine reasonable results. The student is expected to

- **(A)** round two-digit numbers to the nearest ten and three-digit numbers to the nearest hundred; and *(See pages 77–78.)*
- **(B)** estimate sums and differences beyond basic facts. *(See pages 79–80.)*

Name _____   Date _____

Number, Operation, and Quantitative Reasoning

Objective 1

Expectation: use place value to read, write (in symbols and words), and describe the value of whole numbers through 999,999

DIRECTIONS: Choose the best answer.

1. If you arranged these numbers from least to greatest, which number would be last?

1,012   1,022   1,002   1,021

- (A) 1,012
- (B) 1,021
- (C) 1,022
- (D) 1,002

2. Which of these numbers would come before 157 on a number line?

- (F) 159
- (G) 147
- (H) 165
- (J) 158

3. Which of these numbers is nine hundred sixty-four?

- (A) 9,604
- (B) 946
- (C) 9,640
- (D) 964

4. Which group of numbers has three odd numbers?

- (F) 8, 12, 15, 17, 20, 26, 30
- (G) 7, 10, 12, 13, 19, 22, 36
- (H) 2, 5, 8, 14, 18, 28, 32, 40
- (J) 16, 27, 28, 29, 30, 34, 38

5. Which of these is closest in value to 190?

- (A) 186
- (B) 192
- (C) 179
- (D) 199

6. Paul and Vesta used a computer to solve a problem. Which of these is the same as the number on the screen?

- (F) three thousand one hundred eighty
- (G) three hundred eighty
- (H) three thousand one hundred eight
- (J) three thousand eighteen

7. Count by fives. Which number comes after 25 and before 35?

- (A) 50
- (B) 20
- (C) 30
- (D) 40

GO →

Number, Operation, and Quantitative Reasoning

Objective 1

Expectation: use place value to read, write (in symbols and words), and describe the value of whole numbers through 999,999

8. Which of these numbers is eight hundred one thousand, three hundred twenty-two?

   (F) 810,322

   (G) 800,322

   (H) 801,322

   (J) 813,220

9. Which of these is closest in value to 503,561?

   (A) 504,561

   (B) 502,561

   (C) 503,651

   (D) 503,165

10. Which group of numbers has three even numbers?

   (F) 8, 9, 16, 20, 44, 90, 97

   (G) 4, 9, 15, 27, 46, 68, 71

   (H) 3, 21, 44, 66, 75, 83, 93

   (J) 7, 24, 32, 56, 71, 82, 95

11. If you arranged these numbers from greatest to least, which number would be last?

    27,438   27,490   27,432   27,500

   (A) 27,490

   (B) 27,438

   (C) 27,500

   (D) 27,432

12. Which of these numbers is eight hundred ninety five thousand, two hundred forty-nine?

   (F) 895,249

   (G) 8,952.49

   (H) 890,524

   (J) 892,049

13. Count by twos. Which number comes after 2,574 and before 2,588?

   (A) 2,572

   (B) 2,584

   (C) 2,590

   (D) 2,600

14. Which of these is closest in value to 57,240?

   (F) 57,245

   (G) 57,236

   (H) 57,250

   (J) 57,234

15. Which of these numbers would come after 865 on a number line?

   (A) 862

   (B) 855

   (C) 871

   (D) 864

STOP

Number, Operation, and Quantitative Reasoning

Objective 1   **Expectation:** *use place value to compare and order whole numbers through 9,999*

DIRECTIONS: Choose the best answer.

1. **You are ninth in line for movie tickets. How many people are ahead of you?**
   - (A) 9
   - (B) 7
   - (C) 8
   - (D) 10

2. **Which number is greater than 97?**
   - (F) 55
   - (G) 102
   - (H) 87
   - (J) 96

3. **Which of these is closest in value to 2,000?**
   - (A) 1,979
   - (B) 1,997
   - (C) 2,004
   - (D) 2,010

4. **What number is missing from the sequence?**

   6   12   18   _____   30
   - (F) 20
   - (G) 24
   - (H) 22
   - (J) 26

5. **The number 589 is less than _____.**
   - (A) 598
   - (B) 579
   - (C) 589
   - (D) 588

6. **The number 1,691 is less than _____.**
   - (F) 1,609
   - (G) 1,699
   - (H) 1,690
   - (J) 1,600

7. **Count by tens. Which number comes after 70 and before 90?**
   - (A) 50
   - (B) 60
   - (C) 80
   - (D) 100

8. **If a day's snowfall was between 1.01 inches and 2.32 inches, which of the measurements below might be the actual snowfall amount?**
   - (F) 1.00 inch
   - (G) 2.23 inches
   - (H) 2.52 inches
   - (J) 2.60 inches

GO

Number, Operation, and Quantitative Reasoning

Objective 1

Expectation: use place value to compare and order whole numbers through 9,999

---

9. Find the answer that shows 35 peanuts.

Ⓐ

Ⓑ

Ⓒ

Ⓓ

10. The picture below shows the number of cars parked in a lot. Which answer is the same number as is shown in the picture?

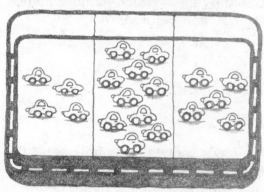

Ⓕ 100 + 40 + 5

Ⓖ 1 + 4 + 5

Ⓗ 400 + 100 + 5

Ⓙ 4 + 10 + 5

11. What number is represented by the chart?

Hundreds	Tens	Ones
l l l	l l l l l	l l l

Ⓐ 335

Ⓑ 533

Ⓒ 353

Ⓓ 335

12. What is another name for 8,488?

Ⓕ 8 thousands, 8 hundreds, 4 tens, 8 ones

Ⓖ 8 thousands, 4 hundreds, 8 tens, 8 ones

Ⓗ 4 thousands, 8 hundreds, 8 tens, 8 ones

Ⓙ 8 thousands, 8 hundreds, 8 tens, 8 ones

13. 8 hundreds and 6 thousands =

Ⓐ 8,600

Ⓑ 8,606

Ⓒ 6,800

Ⓓ 806

STOP

Number, Operation, and Quantitative Reasoning

Objective 1

Expectation: *determine the value of a collection of coins and bills*

Example:

Which answer is the same as $6.28?

- (A) six dollar bills, two dimes, three cents
- (B) six dollar bills, a quarter, three cents
- (C) five dollar bills, five quarters
- (D) five dollar bills, five quarters, a dime

Answer: (B)

---

1. A student bought a pen and received the coins below as change. The pen cost $1.25. How much money did the student give the cashier?

- (A) $1.50
- (B) $1.25
- (C) $1.00
- (D) $0.25

2. How much money is this?

- (F) $0.76
- (G) $0.61
- (H) $0.31
- (J) $26

3. How much money is this?

- (A) $4.70
- (B) $4.85
- (C) $4.97
- (D) $5.07

GO →

Number, Operation, and Quantitative Reasoning

Objective 1 **Expectation:** *determine the value of a collection of coins and bills*

---

4. You have 7 coins that total $0.92. What combination of coins do you have?

   (F) 2 quarters, 2 dimes, 1 nickels, 2 pennies

   (G) 3 quarters, 1 dime, 1 nickel, 2 pennies

   (H) 1 quarter, 3 dimes, 2 nickels, 1 penny

   (J) 2 quarters, 1 dime, 2 nickels, 3 pennies

5. You have 4 coins that total $0.37. What combination of coins do you have?

   (A) 2 quarters, 2 pennies

   (B) 1 quarter, 1 dime, 2 pennies

   (C) 2 dimes, 1 nickel, 1 penny

   (D) 1 quarter, 2 dimes, 2 pennies

6. A sticker costs 20 cents. Jawan has 12 cents. How much more money does he need to buy the sticker?

   (F) $0.08

   (G) $0.10

   (H) $0.12

   (J) $0.32

7. Jawan's sister has four coins. One is a nickel and one is a dime. Which of these amounts might she have?

   (A) 15 cents

   (B) 20 cents

   (C) 24 cents

   (D) 30 cents

8. A single-scoop ice cream cone used to cost $1.39. The price has gone up 9 cents. How much does it cost now?

   (F) $1.42

   (G) $1.48

   (H) $1.58

   (J) $1.30

9. Which combination of coins makes $0.40?

   (A) 1 nickel, 1 dime, 1 half-dollar

   (B) 2 dimes, 1 nickel, 5 pennies

   (C) 3 dimes, 1 nickel, 1 penny

   (D) 1 nickel, 1 dime, 1 quarter

10. Which answer is the same as $5.40?

   (F) one five-dollar bill, two quarters, one dime

   (G) five dollar bills, three dimes, 5 pennies

   (H) four dollar bills, four quarters, 4 dimes

   (J) five dollar bills, 1 quarter, 4 nickel

11. Which combination of coins makes $0.65?

   (A) 1 nickel, 2 quarters, 1 dime

   (B) 1 half-dollar, 1 nickel, 1 penny

   (C) 1 quarter, 5 dimes

   (D) 5 nickels, 1 quarter, 3 dimes

STOP

Number, Operation, and Quantitative Reasoning

Objective 1

Expectation: *compare fractional parts of whole objects or sets of objects in a problem situation using models*

Example:

From the figures below, you know that _____ .

(A) $\frac{3}{4}$ is greater than $\frac{1}{2}$.

(B) $\frac{1}{3}$ is greater than $\frac{1}{2}$.

(C) $\frac{3}{4}$ is less than $\frac{1}{2}$.

(D) $\frac{3}{4}$ is less than $\frac{1}{3}$.

Answer: (B)

DIRECTIONS: Choose the best answer.

1. How much of this figure is shaded?

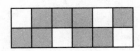

(A) $\frac{3}{4}$

(B) $\frac{2}{3}$

(C) $\frac{1}{3}$

(D) $\frac{3}{10}$

2. $\frac{3}{6} = \frac{\blacksquare}{2}$

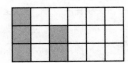

(F) 4

(G) 3

(H) 2

(J) 1

3. If one more block in this figure were shaded, what fraction of the figure would be shaded?

(A) $\frac{1}{6}$

(B) $\frac{1}{3}$

(C) $\frac{1}{2}$

(D) $\frac{2}{3}$

GO

Number, Operation, and Quantitative Reasoning

Objective 1

Expectation: compare fractional parts of whole objects or sets of objects in a problem situation using models

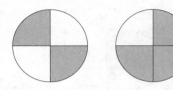

4. From the figures above, you know that—

- (F) $\frac{1}{3}$ is greater than $\frac{2}{3}$
- (G) $\frac{1}{2}$ is greater than $\frac{3}{4}$
- (H) $\frac{1}{2}$ is greater than $\frac{1}{4}$
- (J) $\frac{3}{4}$ is greater than $\frac{1}{2}$

5. Which of these shows a shaded area that is greater than one half?

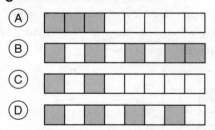

6. In which answer are $\frac{2}{3}$ of the stars shaded?

7. From the figures below, you know that _____.

- (A) $\frac{1}{3}$ is greater than $\frac{2}{3}$
- (B) $\frac{1}{2}$ is greater than $\frac{2}{3}$
- (C) $\frac{2}{3}$ is greater than $\frac{1}{2}$
- (D) $\frac{2}{3}$ is greater than $\frac{1}{3}$

8. From the figures below, you know that _____.

- (F) $\frac{1}{4}$ is greater than $\frac{2}{4}$
- (G) $\frac{1}{2}$ is greater than $\frac{2}{4}$
- (H) $\frac{2}{4}$ is greater than $\frac{1}{4}$
- (J) $\frac{3}{4}$ is greater than $\frac{2}{4}$

STOP

Name _____ Date _____

Number, Operation, and Quantitative Reasoning

Objective 1

Expectation: use fraction names and symbols to describe fractional parts of whole objects or sets of objects with denominators of 12 or less

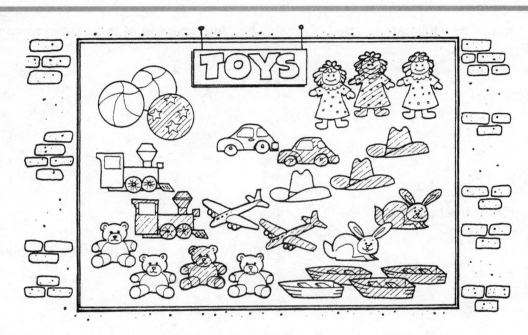

DIRECTIONS: Use the picture of the toy store window to answer the questions.

1. What fraction of the cars are shaded?

   (A) $\frac{1}{2}$

   (B) $\frac{2}{2}$

   (C) $\frac{2}{3}$

   (D) $\frac{1}{3}$

2. What fraction of the teddy bears are shaded?

   (F) $\frac{3}{4}$

   (G) $\frac{1}{3}$

   (H) $\frac{2}{4}$

   (J) $\frac{1}{4}$

3. What fraction of the trains are shaded?

   (A) $\frac{2}{2}$

   (B) $\frac{1}{3}$

   (C) $\frac{1}{2}$

   (D) $\frac{1}{4}$

4. What fraction of the rabbits are shaded?

   (F) $\frac{1}{2}$

   (G) $\frac{2}{2}$

   (H) $\frac{1}{3}$

   (J) $\frac{3}{4}$

GO

Number, Operation, and Quantitative Reasoning

Objective 1

Expectation: *use fraction names and symbols to describe fractional parts of whole objects or sets of objects with denominators of 12 or less*

---

5. What fraction of the dolls are shaded?

   (A) $\frac{2}{3}$

   (B) $\frac{1}{2}$

   (C) $\frac{3}{3}$

   (D) $\frac{1}{3}$

6. What fraction of the hats are shaded?

   (F) $\frac{2}{3}$

   (G) $\frac{1}{3}$

   (H) $\frac{3}{3}$

   (J) $\frac{1}{4}$

7. What fraction of the airplanes are shaded?

   (A) $\frac{1}{3}$

   (B) $\frac{2}{3}$

   (C) $\frac{2}{2}$

   (D) $\frac{1}{2}$

8. What fraction of the boats are shaded?

   (F) $\frac{3}{4}$

   (G) $\frac{1}{4}$

   (H) $\frac{2}{4}$

   (J) $\frac{1}{3}$

9. What fraction of the balls are shaded?

   (A) $\frac{1}{2}$

   (B) $\frac{2}{3}$

   (C) $\frac{1}{3}$

   (D) $\frac{3}{3}$

STOP

Name _____ Date _____

Number, Operation, and Quantitative Reasoning

Objective 1

Expectation: *model addition and subtraction using pictures, words, and numbers*

 Clue   When you are not sure about a subtraction answer, check it by adding.

DIRECTIONS: Mark the space for the correct answer to each addition and subtraction problem. Choose "None of these" if the right answer is not given.

1. 39 + 21 =
   - (A) 59
   - (B) 61
   - (C) 65
   - (D) None of these

2.   299
     + 54
   - (F) 335
   - (G) 353
   - (H) 355
   - (J) None of these

3. 12 + 29 + 6 =
   - (A) 45
   - (B) 49
   - (C) 47
   - (D) None of these

4.   519
     +56
   - (F) 575
   - (G) 557
   - (H) 577
   - (J) None of these

5.   270
     955
     +116
   - (A) 1,343
   - (B) 1,431
   - (C) 1,340
   - (D) None of these

6.   62
     −17
   - (F) 44
   - (G) 46
   - (H) 45
   - (J) None of these

GO →

Number, Operation, and Quantitative Reasoning

Objective 1

Expectation: model addition and subtraction using pictures, words, and numbers

---

7. 200
    −80
    - (A) 30
    - (B) 10
    - (C) 20
    - (D) None of these

8. 444 − 44 − 4 =
    - (F) 440
    - (G) 436
    - (H) 410
    - (J) None of these

9. There are 762 CD titles listed in the music store's computer. Marcy entered 292 new titles into the computer. What is the total number of CD titles listed now?
    - (A) 954
    - (B) 1054
    - (C) 470
    - (D) 1154

10. One day 278 CDs were sold. The next day 183 CDs were sold. What is the total number of CDs sold in those two days?
    - (F) 461
    - (G) 95
    - (H) 361
    - (J) 561

11. Steve walked a total of 18 blocks the day he went to the water park with Todd. If he walked 3 blocks to Todd's house then 6 blocks to the park, how many blocks did he walk when he went home later that night?
    - (A) 27
    - (B) 6
    - (C) 9
    - (D) 18

12. A total of 853 tickets were sold at the water park on Wednesday and Thursday. If 435 tickets were sold on Wednesday, how many tickets were sold on Thursday?
    - (F) 318
    - (G) 481
    - (H) 418
    - (J) 1288

STOP

Number, Operation, and Quantitative Reasoning

Objective 1

Expectation: select addition or subtraction and use the operation to solve problems involving whole numbers through 999

Example:

What number completes the number sentence ■ + 0 = 5?

- (A) 0
- (B) 5
- (C) 10
- (D) 50

Answer: (B)

DIRECTIONS: Choose the best answer.

1. What number completes both of the number sentences below?

    21 − ■ = 17   8 + ■ = 12

    - (A) 4
    - (B) 5
    - (C) 9
    - (D) 13

2. What sign belongs in the circle in the number sentence below?

    10 − 1 = 7 ■ 2

    - (F) −
    - (G) +
    - (H) ×
    - (J) ÷

3. What should replace the ■ in the number sentence below?

    20 + ■ = 20

    - (A) 0
    - (B) 1
    - (C) 20
    - (D) 100

4. Which number, if placed in both boxes will make the number sentence below true?   8 + ■ + ■ = 30

    - (F) 9
    - (G) 11
    - (H) 22
    - (J) 38

GO

Number, Operation, and Quantitative Reasoning

Objective 1

Expectation: select addition or subtraction and use the operation to solve problems involving whole numbers through 999

---

5. Athletic shoes normally cost $50. The price was reduced by $10. What is the new price of the shoes?

- (A) $50 + $10 = ■
- (B) $50 − $10 = ■
- (C) $50 × $10 = ■
- (D) $50 ÷ $10 = ■

6. A researcher studied 17 frogs. Eight of them were leopard frogs. How many of them were not leopard frogs?

- (F) 8
- (G) 9
- (H) 25
- (J) Not Here

7. The trip from Homeville to Lincoln usually takes 25 minutes by car. While making the trip, a driver spent 12 minutes getting gas and 5 minutes waiting for a road crew. How long did it take the driver to make the trip?

- (A) 32 minutes
- (B) 37 minutes
- (C) 48 minutes
- (D) 42 minutes

8. The price of bread was $1.29 but was increased by 8 cents. What was the new price of the bread?

- (F) $1.21
- (G) $1.36
- (H) $1.37
- (J) $1.39

9. The level of a pond dropped 37 inches below normal during a dry spell. It then rose 11 inches because of heavy rains. How far below normal was it?

- (A) 24 inches
- (B) 26 inches
- (C) 48 inches
- (D) Not Here

10. A farmer planted 18 acres on Monday, 29 on Tuesday, and 27 on Wednesday. How many acres did she plant all together?

- (F) 56
- (G) 64
- (H) 73
- (J) 74

11. The marching band had fund-raisers for new uniforms. They made $395.00 on candy sales, $233.00 on wrapping paper sales, and $185.00 on a car wash. How much money did the band raise all together?

- (A) $813.00
- (B) $628.00
- (C) $418.00
- (D) $831.00

STOP

Name _____ Date _____

Number, Operation, and Quantitative Reasoning

Objective 1

Expectation: solve and record multiplication problems (one-digit multiplier)

DIRECTIONS: Choose the best answer. Choose "None of these" if the answer is not given.

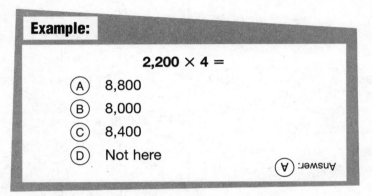

Example:

2,200 × 4 =

- (A) 8,800
- (B) 8,000
- (C) 8,400
- (D) Not here

Answer: (A)

Clue

Before working the problem, estimate the answer. Then eliminate answers that are not close to the estimate.

1. 220 × 4 =
   - (A) 880
   - (B) 800
   - (C) 840
   - (D) None of these

2. 3,000 × 5 =
   - (F) 5,000
   - (G) 18,000
   - (H) 15,000
   - (J) None of these

3. 410 × 6 =
   - (A) 2,466
   - (B) 2,460
   - (C) 2,465
   - (D) None of these

4. 9,000 × 5 =
   - (F) 45,000
   - (G) 4,500
   - (H) 36,000
   - (J) None of these

5. 311 × 2 =
   - (A) 722
   - (B) 522
   - (C) 622
   - (D) None of these

6. 7,000 × 7 =
   - (F) 42,000
   - (G) 56,000
   - (H) 45,000
   - (J) None of these

GO

Number, Operation, and Quantitative Reasoning

Objective
1

Expectation: *solve and record multiplication problems (one-digit multiplier)*

---

7. 618 × 7 =
- (A) 4,326
- (B) 4,426
- (C) 4,246
- (D) None of these

8. 999 × 9 =
- (F) 8,991
- (G) 6,993
- (H) 7,992
- (J) None of these

9. 4,300 × 4 =
- (A) 4,700
- (B) 16,200
- (C) 17,200
- (D) None of these

10. 150 × 8 =
- (F) 813
- (G) 1,200
- (H) 1400
- (J) None of these

11. 430 × 8 =
- (A) 438
- (B) 3,440
- (C) 3,224
- (D) None of these

12. 575 × 3 =
- (F) 725
- (G) 1,705
- (H) 1,575
- (J) None of these

13. 5,000 × 4 =
- (A) 20,000
- (B) 2,000
- (C) 200,000
- (D) None of these

14. 8000 × 2 =
- (F) 4,000
- (G) 160,000
- (H) 16,000
- (J) None of these

15. 2,100 × 6 =
- (A) 1,260
- (B) 12,600
- (C) 18,000
- (D) None of these

16. 529 × 7 =
- (F) 3,503
- (G) 3,703
- (H) 37,030
- (J) None of these

STOP

Number, Operation, and Quantitative Reasoning

Objective 1

Expectation: *use models to solve division problems and use number sentences to record the solutions*

DIRECTIONS: Choose the best answer. Choose "None of these" if the answer is not given.

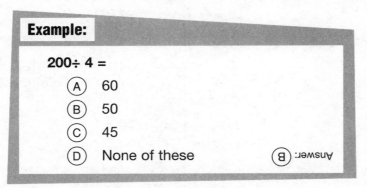

Example:

200 ÷ 4 =

- (A) 60
- (B) 50
- (C) 45
- (D) None of these

Answer: (B)

Clue — When you are not sure of an answer, check it by multiplying.

DIRECTIONS: Choose the best answer. Choose "None of these" if the answer is not given.

1. 100 ÷ 10 =
   - (A) 10
   - (B) 100
   - (C) 1
   - (D) None of these

2. 426 ÷ 6 =
   - (F) 61
   - (G) 51
   - (H) 71
   - (J) None of these

3. 135 ÷ 5 =
   - (A) 71
   - (B) 17
   - (C) 27
   - (D) None of these

4. 490 ÷ 7 =
   - (F) 70
   - (G) 60
   - (H) 50
   - (J) None of these

5. 880 ÷ 2 =
   - (A) 401
   - (B) 440
   - (C) 400
   - (D) None of these

6. 160 ÷ 8 =
   - (F) 30
   - (G) 24
   - (H) 48
   - (J) None of these

GO

Number, Operation, and Quantitative Reasoning

Objective 1

Expectation: *use models to solve division problems and use number sentences to record the solutions*

---

7. $9\overline{)189}$

- (A) 21
- (B) 31
- (C) 41
- (D) None of these

8. $555 \div 5 =$

- (F) 11
- (G) 100
- (H) 101
- (J) None of these

9. $200 \div 4 =$

- (A) 60
- (B) 50
- (C) 45
- (D) None of these

10. $10\overline{)220}$

- (F) 22
- (G) 11
- (H) 21
- (J) None of these

11. $6\overline{)936}$

- (A) 166
- (B) 156
- (C) 5,616
- (D) None of these

12. $690 \div 2 =$

- (F) 340
- (G) 345
- (H) 445
- (J) None of these

13. $750 \div 3$

- (A) 350
- (B) 215
- (C) 250
- (D) None of these

14. $990 \div 3 =$

- (F) 330
- (G) 327
- (H) 270
- (J) None of these

15. $210 \div 7 =$

- (A) 33
- (B) 300
- (C) 30
- (D) None of these

16. $4\overline{)600}$

- (F) 165
- (G) 160
- (H) 195
- (J) None of these

STOP

Name _____ Date _____

Number, Operation, and Quantitative Reasoning

Objective 1

Expectation: round two-digit numbers to the nearest ten and three-digit numbers to the nearest hundred

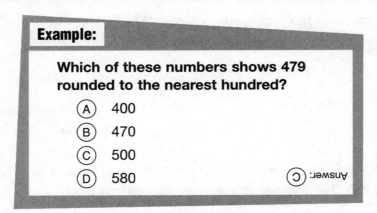

Example:

Which of these numbers shows 479 rounded to the nearest hundred?

(A) 400

(B) 470

(C) 500

(D) 580

Answer: C

DIRECTIONS: Choose the best answer.

1. **Round to the nearest hundred.**
   Example: For 350 and up, round to 400.
   For 349 and down, round to 300.

   921 _____ 662 _____ 882 _____

   458 _____ 187 _____ 363 _____

   393 _____ 527 _____ 211 _____

2. **Round to nearest thousand.**
   Example: For 6,500 and up, round to 7,000. For 6,499 and down, round to 6,000.

   2,495 _____ 3,379 _____ 4,289 _____

   7,001 _____ 8,821 _____ 6,213 _____

   5,111 _____ 9,339 _____ 2,985 _____

3. **Which of these numbers is 288 rounded to the nearest hundred?**

   (A) 200

   (B) 300

   (C) 280

   (D) 380

4. **Round these numbers to the nearest hundred: 575, 612, 499, 633, 590, 680. How many of them will be 600?**

   (F) 3

   (G) 4

   (H) 5

   (J) 6

GO

Number, Operation, and Quantitative Reasoning

Objective 1

Expectation: *round two-digit numbers to the nearest ten and three-digit numbers to the nearest hundred*

5. **Which of these numbers is 587 rounded to the nearest hundred?**
   - (A) 580
   - (B) 500
   - (C) 690
   - (D) 600

6. **Round these numbers to the nearest ten: 179, 225, 212, 141, 255, 149. How many of them will round to 210?**
   - (F) 0
   - (G) 1
   - (H) 2
   - (J) 3

7. **Which of these is 647 rounded to the nearest hundred?**
   - (A) 500
   - (B) 600
   - (C) 700
   - (D) 650

8. **Round these numbers to the nearest hundred: 749, 832, 845, 775, 751, 725. How many of them will be 800?**
   - (F) 3
   - (G) 4
   - (H) 5
   - (J) 6

9. **Which of these is 4,485 rounded to the nearest hundred?**
   - (A) 4,500
   - (B) 5,000
   - (C) 4,000
   - (D) 4,400

10. **Which of these is 849 rounded to the nearest ten?**
    - (F) 850
    - (G) 845
    - (H) 840
    - (J) 800

11. **Round these numbers to the nearest thousand.**

    3,495 _____   2,449 _____   9,820 _____

    6,200 _____   5,499 _____   2,401 _____

    1,099 _____   4,713 _____   8,683 _____

12. **Round these numbers to the nearest ten: 175, 144, 136, 142, 133, 146. How many of them will round to 140?**
    - (A) 3
    - (B) 4
    - (C) 5
    - (D) 6

STOP

Name _____ Date _____

Number, Operation, and Quantitative Reasoning

Objective 1

Expectation: estimate sums and differences beyond basic facts

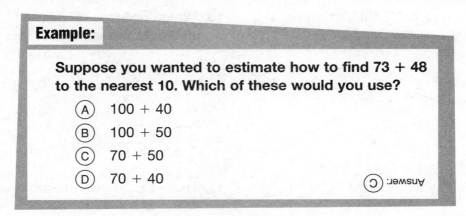

Example:

Suppose you wanted to estimate how to find 73 + 48 to the nearest 10. Which of these would you use?

Ⓐ   100 + 40

Ⓑ   100 + 50

Ⓒ   70 + 50

Ⓓ   70 + 40

Answer: Ⓒ

DIRECTIONS: Choose the best answer.

1. **Which of these is the best way to estimate the answer to this problem?**

   286 − 109 = ▓

   Ⓐ   300 − 100 = ▓

   Ⓑ   200 − 100 = ▓

   Ⓒ   300 − 200 = ▓

   Ⓓ   100 − 100 = ▓

2. **Which number sentence would you use to estimate 97 + 9 to the nearest 10?**

   Ⓕ   90 + 5

   Ⓖ   100 + 10

   Ⓗ   90 + 10

   Ⓙ   100 + 5

3. **Use estimation to find which of these is closest to 1000.**

   Ⓐ   591 + 573

   Ⓑ   499 + 409

   Ⓒ   392 + 589

   Ⓓ   913 + 183

4. **A group of people brought their pets to a street fair. 33 people brought dogs and 18 people brought cats. If 11 people brought other kinds of pets, which of these is closest to the number of people who brought pets?**

   Ⓕ   50

   Ⓖ   60

   Ⓗ   70

   Ⓙ   80

5. **Michael was at a card convention. At the first booth he bought 8 cards. He bought 6 cards at the next booth and 3 at the last booth. Which of these is closest to the number of cards Michael bought?**

   Ⓐ   5

   Ⓑ   10

   Ⓒ   15

   Ⓓ   20

GO

Number, Operation, and Quantitative Reasoning

Objective 1

Expectation: estimate sums and differences beyond basic facts

6. Use estimation to find which of these is closest to 800.
   - (F) 325 + 267
   - (G) 456 + 267
   - (H) 782 + 151
   - (J) 293 + 421

7. Which of these is the best way to estimate the answer to this problem?
   426 − 258 = ■
   - (A) 400 − 300 = ■
   - (B) 400 − 200 = ■
   - (C) 500 − 200 = ■
   - (D) 500 − 300 = ■

8. Which number sentence would you use to estimate the problem?
   137 + 59 = ■
   - (F) 200 + 100 = ■
   - (G) 100 + 100 = ■
   - (H) 150 + 100 = ■
   - (J) 150 + 60 = ■

9. Use estimation to find which of these is closest to 300.
   - (A) 138 + 165
   - (B) 283 + 51
   - (C) 128 + 97
   - (D) 148 + 142

10. Which of these is the best way to estimate the answer to this problem?
    459 − 220 = ■
    - (F) 500 − 300 = ■
    - (G) 400 − 300 = ■
    - (H) 400 − 200 = ■
    - (J) 500 − 200 = ■

11. Use estimation to find out which of these is closest to 500.
    - (A) 751 − 231 = ■
    - (B) 735 − 249 = ■
    - (C) 602 − 153 = ■
    - (D) 593 − 170 = ■

12. Which number sentence would you use to estimate the problem?
    1,498 − 575 = ■
    - (F) 1,400 − 600 = ■
    - (G) 2,000 − 500 = ■
    - (H) 1,500 − 600 = ■
    - (J) 1,000 − 500 = ■

13. Use estimation to find out which of these is closest to 400.
    - (A) 245 + 45
    - (B) 266 + 95
    - (C) 152 + 252
    - (D) 380 + 120

STOP

Objective

1

Mini-Test

DIRECTIONS: Choose the best answer.

1. **Count by tens. Which number comes after 70 and before 90?**
   - (A) 50
   - (B) 60
   - (C) 80
   - (D) 100

2. **Which answer is the same as $1.23?**
   - (F) one dollar bill, one quarter, three pennies
   - (G) one dollar bill, two dimes, three pennies
   - (H) five quarters, three pennies
   - (J) one dollar bill, two dimes, one nickel

3. **In which answer are $\frac{1}{4}$ of the stars shaded?**
   - (A)
   - (B)
   - (C)
   - (D)

4. **What fraction of the**  **'s are raining?**

   - (F) $\frac{1}{3}$
   - (G) $\frac{2}{3}$
   - (H) $\frac{1}{4}$
   - (J) $\frac{1}{2}$

5. **Sandy had 5**

   She read 2

   Find the number sentence that tells how many books Sandy has left to read.
   - (A) $5 + 2 = 7$
   - (B) $5 - 2 = 3$
   - (C) $2 + 3 = 5$
   - (D) $2 - 1 = 1$

6. **What number completes the number sentence ■ + 4 = 17?**
   - (F) 17
   - (G) 4
   - (H) 13
   - (J) 3

7. **249 × 5 =**
   - (A) 1,245
   - (B) 254
   - (C) 425
   - (D) 120

8. **10 ÷ 2 =**
   - (F) 2
   - (G) 4
   - (H) 5
   - (J) None of these

STOP

TAKS Mathematics—Objective 2

The student will demonstrate an understanding of patterns, relationships, and algebraic reasoning.

(3.6) Patterns, relationships, and algebraic thinking

The student uses patterns to solve problems. The student is expected to

(A) identify and extend whole-number and geometric patterns to make predictions and solve problems; *(See pages 83–84.)*

(B) identify patterns in multiplication facts using [concrete objects,] pictorial models, [or technology]; and *(See pages 85–86.)*

(C) identify patterns in related multiplication and division sentences (fact families) such as $2 \times 3 = 6$, $3 \times 2 = 6$, $6 \div 2 = 3$, $6 \div 3 = 2$. *(See pages 87–88.)*

(3.7) Patterns, relationships, and algebraic thinking

The student uses lists, tables, and charts to express patterns and relationships. The student is expected to

(A) generate a table of paired numbers based on a real-life situation such as insects and legs; and *(See pages 89–90.)*

(B) identify patterns in a table of related number pairs based on a real-life situation and extend the table. *(See pages 91–92.)*

What it means:

- A table of paired numbers shows a relationship between two sets of numbers. For example, a table might show that one dog has four legs, so two dogs would have eight legs, three dogs would have twelve legs, and so forth.

Patterns, Relationships, and Algebraic Thinking

Objective 2

Expectation: *identify and extend whole-number and geometric patterns to make predictions and solve problems*

Example:

What number is missing from the sequence?

6	12	18		30

(A) 20

(B) 24

(C) 22

(D) 26

Answer: (B)

DIRECTIONS: Choose the best answer.

1. What number is missing from the sequence?

3	6		12	15

(A) 8

(B) 9

(C) 10

(D) 11

2. What number is missing from the sequence?

11	22		44	55

(F) 33

(G) 23

(H) 66

(J) 42

3. Look at the pattern below. Which grouping is missing from the pattern?

(A)

(B)

(C)

(D)

GO

Patterns, Relationships, and Algebraic Thinking

Objective 2

Expectation: identify and extend whole-number and geometric patterns to make predictions and solve problems

---

4. What number is missing from the sequence?

429	433	437	441	

- (F) 443
- (G) 444
- (H) 445
- (J) 447

5. What number is missing from the sequence?

7	16	25	34		52

- (A) 38
- (B) 39
- (C) 42
- (D) 43

6. What number is missing from the sequence?

8	16	24	

- (F) 28
- (G) 30
- (H) 32
- (J) 34

7. What number is missing from the sequence?

37	31		22	19

- (A) 24
- (B) 25
- (C) 26
- (D) 27

8. What number is missing from the sequence?

120	108	98	90	

- (F) 84
- (G) 85
- (H) 86
- (J) 87

9. What number is missing from the sequence?

2	3	5	6	8	9	11	

- (A) 12
- (B) 13
- (C) 14
- (D) 15

STOP

Name _____ Date _____

Patterns, Relationships, and Algebraic Thinking

Objective 2

Expectation: identify patterns in multiplication facts using pictorial models

---

DIRECTIONS: Choose the number sentence that means the same as the picture, description, and number sentence given in questions 1–4.

1. 3 circles in 2 groups

3 + 3

Ⓐ 3 × 3

Ⓑ 3 × 2

Ⓒ 2 × 2

Ⓓ 6 × 2

2. 4 squares in 4 groups

4 + 4 + 4 + 4

Ⓕ 8 × 4

Ⓖ 8 × 8

Ⓗ 4 × 4

Ⓙ 4 × 2

3. 5 triangles in 2 groups

5 + 5

Ⓐ 5 × 2

Ⓑ 5 × 5

Ⓒ 2 × 2

Ⓓ 5 × 1

4. 4 stars in 3 groups

4 + 4 + 4

Ⓕ 4 × 4

Ⓖ 4 × 4

Ⓗ 12 × 3

Ⓙ 4 × 3

GO →

Patterns, Relationships, and Algebraic Thinking

Objective 2

Expectation: *identify patterns in multiplication facts using pictorial models*

DIRECTIONS: For exercises 5-9, write the description and draw the multiplication problem shown.

5. 3 × 3

6. 6 × 1

7. 7 × 2

8. 4 × 5

9. 6 × 1

STOP

Name _____ Date _____

Patterns, Relationships, and Algebraic Thinking

Objective 2

Expectation: identify patterns in related multiplication and division sentences (fact families)

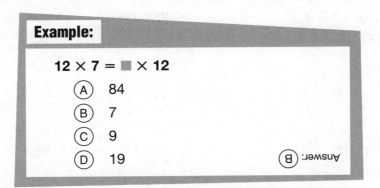

Example:

$12 \times 7 = \blacksquare \times 12$

- (A) 84
- (B) 7
- (C) 9
- (D) 19

Answer: (B)

DIRECTIONS: Choose the best answer.

1. $32 \div 16 = 2$; $16 \times \blacksquare = 32$
   - (A) 32
   - (B) 16
   - (C) 2
   - (D) 8

2. $12 \times 10 = \blacksquare \times 12$
   - (F) 10
   - (G) 12
   - (H) 120
   - (J) 2

3. $(10 \times 5) \times 6 = \blacksquare \times (5 \times 6)$
   - (A) 50
   - (B) 30
   - (C) 300
   - (D) 10

4. $7.5 \times 3.8 = 3.8 \times \blacksquare$
   - (F) 28.5
   - (G) 7.5
   - (H) 3.8
   - (J) 3.7

5. $(6 \times 8) \times 5 = 6 \times (8 \times \blacksquare)$
   - (A) 45
   - (B) 53
   - (C) 5
   - (D) 48

6. $25 \div 5 = \blacksquare$; $5 \times \blacksquare = 25$
   - (F) 5
   - (G) 25
   - (H) 50
   - (J) 10

GO

Patterns, Relationships, and Algebraic Thinking

Objective 2

Expectation: *identify patterns in related multiplication and division sentences (fact families)*

---

7. 24 × (12 × 12) = (24 × 12) × ▪

- (A) 24
- (B) 12
- (C) 144
- (D) 3,456

8. 81 ÷ 9 = ▪; 9 × ▪ = 81

- (F) 3
- (G) 81
- (H) 12
- (J) 9

9. 7 × 5 × 4 = (7 × 4) × ▪

- (A) 5
- (B) 20
- (C) 4
- (D) 35

10. 144 ÷ 12 = ▪; 12 × ▪ = 144

- (F) 48
- (G) 14
- (H) 24
- (J) 12

11. 9 × (7 × 3) = (9 × ▪) × 3

- (A) 7
- (B) 21
- (C) 63
- (D) 27

12. 56 ÷ 14 = ▪; 14 × ▪ = 56

- (F) 6
- (G) 4
- (H) 8
- (J) 9

13. 23.7 × 56.4 = 56.4 × ▪

- (A) 23.7
- (B) 27.3
- (C) 36.68
- (D) 56.4

14. (26 × 13) × 13 = 26 × (13 × ▪)

- (F) 169
- (G) 39
- (H) 26
- (J) 13

15. 64 ÷ 8 = ▪; 8 × ▪ = 64

- (A) 9
- (B) 8
- (C) 12
- (D) 56

16. 24 × 4 × 8 = (8 × 24) × ▪

- (F) 3
- (G) 4
- (H) 12
- (J) 9

STOP

Patterns, Relationships, and Algebraic Thinking

Objective 2

Expectation: generate a table of paired numbers based on a real-life situation such as insects and legs

---

DIRECTIONS: Choose the best table.

1. Bill is helping to make a large fruit salad for the school fund-raiser. He needs to go to the grocery store to get 6 pounds of grapes. One pound of grapes costs $1.20. How much money should Bill take with him?

(A)

Pounds of Grapes	1	2	3	4	5	6
Amount	$1.20	$2.00	$3.20	$4.00	$5.20	$6.00

(B)

Pounds of Grapes	1	2	3	4	5	6
Amount	$1.20	$2.20	$3.20	$4.20	$5.20	$6.20

(C)

Pounds of Grapes	1	2	3	4	5	6
Amount	$1.20	$2.40	$3.60	$4.80	$6.00	$7.20

(D)

Pounds of Grapes	1	2	3	4	5	6
Amount	$1.20	$3.20	$4.00	$5.20	$5.60	$7.60

2. The weatherman predicted that the temperature would drop 3 degrees every hour between 1:00 A.M. and 6:00 A.M. If it is 54 degrees at 1:00 A.M., what will the temperature be at 6:00 A.M.?

(F)

Time	1:00	2:00	3:00	4:00	5:00	6:00
Temperature	54°	51°	48°	45°	42°	39°

(G)

Time	1:00	2:00	3:00	4:00	5:00	6:00
Temperature	54°	57°	60°	63°	66°	69°

(H)

Time	1:00	2:00	3:00	4:00	5:00	6:00
Temperature	54°	51°	48°	46°	43°	40°

(J)

Time	1:00	2:00	3:00	4:00	5:00	6:00
Temperature	54°	53°	50°	47°	44°	41°

GO

Patterns, Relationships, and Algebraic Thinking

Objective 2

Expectation: generate a table of paired numbers based on a real-life situation such as insects and legs

3. Joshua counted 9 starfish in a tank at the Aquarium. If each starfish had five arms, how many starfish arms were in the tank all together?

(A)

Starfish	1	2	3	4	5	6	7	8	9
Arms	5	10	15	20	25	30	35	40	45

(B)

Starfish	1	2	3	4	5	6	7	8	9
Arms	5	10	20	25	30	40	45	50	55

(C)

Starfish	1	2	3	4	5	6	7	8	9
Arms	1	5	10	15	20	25	30	35	40

(D)

Starfish	1	2	3	4	5	6	7	8	9
Arms	4	8	12	16	20	24	28	32	36

4. Barbara saw 9 antique cars in the parade. What was the total number of wheels on the antique cars?

(F)

Cars	1	2	3	4	5	6	7	8	9
Wheels	4	5	6	7	8	9	10	11	12

(G)

Cars	1	2	3	4	5	6	7	8	9
Wheels	4	8	10	12	16	20	24	28	32

(H)

Cars	1	2	3	4	5	6	7	8	9
Wheels	3	6	9	12	15	18	21	24	27

(J)

Cars	1	2	3	4	5	6	7	8	9
Wheels	4	8	12	16	20	24	28	32	36

STOP

Patterns, Relationships, and Algebraic Thinking

Objective
2

Expectation: identify patterns in a table of related number pairs based on real-life situation and extend the table

---

Examples:

What is the total cost of 6 gallons of gasoline if 1 gallon costs $1.10?

Gallons	1	2	3	4	5	6
Price	$1.10	$2.20	$3.30	$4.40	$5.50	

- (A) $1.16
- (B) $6.06
- (C) $6.60
- (D) None of these

Answer: (C)

DIRECTIONS: Choose the best answer to complete each table.

1. Sheri, Amir, and Paolo each bought a snack cake for $.35. How much did they spend all together for snack cakes?

Snack Cakes	1	2	3
Price	$.35	$.70	

- (A) $.38
- (B) $1.05
- (C) $1.15
- (D) $.70

2. Four families each gave $20 to charity. How much money did they give all together?

Families	1	2	3	4
Amount	$20.00	$40.00	$60.00	

- (F) $24
- (G) $60
- (H) $84
- (J) $80

Patterns, Relationships, and Algebraic Thinking

Objective 2

Expectation: generate a table of paired numbers based on a real-life situation such as insects and legs

3. **A postal worker walks 16 miles in a day. How far does the worker walk in 6 days?**

Days	1	2	3	4	5	6
Miles	16	32	48	64	80	

- (A) 12 miles
- (B) 20 miles
- (C) 96 miles
- (D) 99 miles

4. **There are 8 students on each team. What is the total number of arms and legs on a team?**

Students	1	2	3	4	5	6	7	8
Arms and Legs	4	8	12	16	20	24		

- (F) 28, 32
- (G) 24, 28
- (H) 26, 30
- (J) 32, 34

5. **A pet store owner had 18 fish. He had 3 tanks and wanted to put the same number of fish in each tank. How many fish would he put in each tank?**

Tanks	1	2	3	4	5	6	7
Fish	7	14	21				

- (A) $18 + 3 = $ ▪
- (B) $18 - 3 = $ ▪
- (C) $18 \div 3 = $ ▪
- (D) $18 \times 3 = $ ▪

STOP

Objective
2

Mini-Test

DIRECTIONS: Choose the best answer.

1. **What shape is missing from this pattern?**

   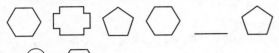

   (A) ⬡

   (B) ⬠

   (C) ▯

   (D) Not Here

2. **Ricky carried 4 boxes of tiles into the kitchen. Each box held 12 tiles. What would you do to find out how many tiles he carried into the kitchen all together?**

   (F) add

   (G) subtract

   (H) divide

   (J) multiply

3. **There were 85 boxes shipped to the warehouse. In each box there were 22 cartons. In each carton there were 40 water guns. How many water guns are in all 85 boxes?**

   (A) 880 water guns

   (B) 1,870 water guns

   (C) 74,800 water guns

   (D) Not Here

4. **What other equation belongs in the same fact family as 17 × 8 = 136?**

   (F) $8 \times 136 = 1,088$

   (G) $136 \div 2 = 68$

   (H) $8 \times 17 = 136$

   (J) $17 + 8 = 25$

5. **What other equation belongs in the same fact family as 136 ÷ 2 = 68?**

   (A) $2 \times 68 = 136$

   (B) $2 + 68 = 70$

   (C) $136 - 68 = 68$

   (D) $136 - 82 = 134$

6. **Jimmy wants to buy baseball cards for his collection. At a sale, the cards are being sold in packs.**

Number of Packs	Number of Cards
2	16
4	32
6	?
7	56

   What is the missing number in the chart?

   (F) 38

   (G) 42

   (H) 48

   (J) Not Here

STOP

TAKS Mathematics—Objective 3

The student will demonstrate an understanding of geometry and spatial reasoning.

(3.8) Geometry and spatial reasoning

The student uses formal geometric vocabulary. The student is expected to

(A) name, describe, and compare shapes and solids using formal geometric vocabulary. *(See pages 95–96.)*

(3.9) Geometry and spatial reasoning

The student recognizes congruence and symmetry. The student is expected to

(A) identify congruent shapes; and *(See pages 97–98.)*

(C) identify lines of symmetry in shapes. *(See pages 99–100.)*

What it means:

- Two figures are congruent if they are the same size and shape.
- A line of symmetry is the line that divides a figure into two mirror images.

(3.10) Geometry and spatial reasoning

The student recognizes that numbers can be represented by points on a line. The student is expected to

(A) locate and name points on a line using whole numbers [and fractions such as halves]. *(See pages 101–102.)*

Name _____ Date _____

Geometry and Spatial Reasoning

Objective 3

Expectation: *name, describe, and compare shapes and solids using formal geometric vocabulary*

Example:

This shape is called a(n) _____.

  (A) pentagon

  (B) hexagon

  (C) octagon

  (D) triangle

Answer: (C)

 Clue   Think of objects, such as stop signs, to help you remember the different shapes.

DIRECTIONS: Choose the best answer.

1. A four-sided figure could be a _____.

  (A) circle

  (B) triangle

  (C) square

  (D) pentagon

2. This shape is called a _____.

  (F) circle

  (G) sphere

  (H) pentagon

  (J) pyramid

3. Which polygon has more sides then a hexagon?

  (A) pentagon

  (B) triangle

  (C) octagon

  (D) square

4. A polygon that has 6 sides and 6 vertices is a _____.

  (F) pentagon

  (G) hexagon

  (H) octagon

  (J) trapezoid

GO

Geometry and Spatial Reasoning

Objective 3

Expectation: *name, describe, and compare shapes and solids using formal geometric vocabulary*

---

5. What is the perimeter of the polygon?

   (A) 38 inches

   (B) 26 inches

   (C) 28 inches

   (D) 37 inches

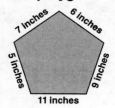

6. How many sides does a quadrilateral have?

   (F) 3

   (G) 4

   (H) 5

   (J) 6

7. A cereal box is shaped like a _____.

   (A) pyramid

   (B) sphere

   (C) rectangular prism

   (D) cone

8. An alphabet block is usually shaped like a _____.

   (F) pyramid

   (G) cone

   (H) cylinder

   (J) cube

9. A can of soup is shaped like a _____.

   (A) pyramid

   (B) sphere

   (C) cylinder

   (D) trapezoid

10. What is this shape?

   (F) cone

   (G) sphere

   (H) cylinder

   (J) cube

11. What is this shape?

   (A) cone

   (B) sphere

   (C) cylinder

   (D) cube

12. What is this shape?

   (F) cone

   (G) sphere

   (H) cylinder

   (J) cube

STOP

Name _____ Date _____

Geometry and Spatial Reasoning

Objective
3

Expectation: identify congruent shapes

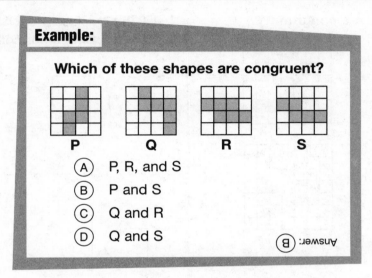
DIRECTIONS: Choose the best answer.

1. **One of these figures is not congruent with the others. Which one is it?**

   Ⓐ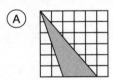

   Ⓑ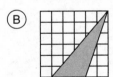

   Ⓒ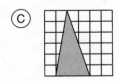

   Ⓓ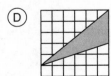

2. **Which of these figures is not the same shape and size as the others?**

   Ⓕ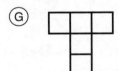

   Ⓖ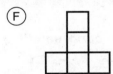

   Ⓗ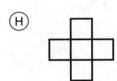

   Ⓙ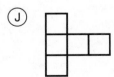

GO ⇒

Geometry and Spatial Reasoning

Objective 3

Expectation: *identify congruent shapes*

---

3. Which two shapes are congruent?

M
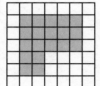

N

O
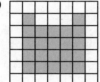

P

- (A) M and N
- (B) O and M
- (C) N and O
- (D) P and M

4. Which two circles are congruent?

F

G

H

J

- (F) H and J
- (G) G and H
- (H) F and H
- (J) F and J

DIRECTIONS: Classify each pair below as **congruent**, **similar**, or **neither.**

5.
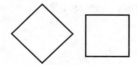

_____

6.

_____

7.
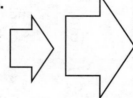

_____

8.

_____

STOP

Geometry and Spatial Reasoning

Objective 3

Expectation: *identify lines of symmetry in shapes*

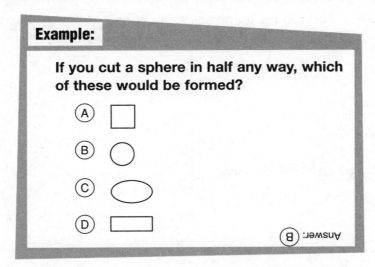

Example:

If you cut a sphere in half any way, which of these would be formed?

- (A) ▢
- (B) ○
- (C) ⬯
- (D) ▭

Answer: (B)

---

1. Which of these shapes can be folded along the dotted line so the parts match?

   (A)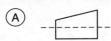

   (B)

   (C)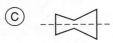

   (D) ⬚

2. Which of the following words has a line of symmetry?
   - (F) DECK
   - (G) CAR
   - (H) BOAT
   - (J) TOWN

3. Which of the following words has a line of symmetry?
   - (A) SIT
   - (B) SCHOOL
   - (C) FOOT
   - (D) MOM

4. Which of the following shows the other half of this object?

   - (F) ⊐
   - (G) ⊐
   - (H) ⊏
   - (J) ⊏

GO →

Geometry and
Spatial Reasoning

Objective
3

Expectation: *identify lines of symmetry in shapes*

---

5. **Which of the following words have a line of symmetry?**

   (A) LINE

   (B) BOOK

   (C) AND

   (D) USED

6. **Which of these letters is *not* symmetrical?**

   (F) H

   (G) O

   (H) Z

   (J) X

7. **Which of these letters is symmetrical?**

   (A) S

   (B) P

   (C) Q

   (D) W

8. **Which of these shapes does not have a line of symmetry?**

   (F)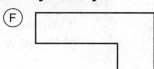

   (G)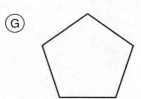

   (H)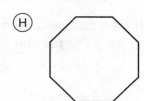

   (J)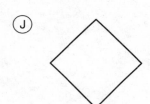

STOP

Geometry and Spatial Reasoning

Objective 3

Expectation: locate and name points on a line using whole numbers

DIRECTIONS: Choose the best answer. Use the number line for the example and exercises 1–4.

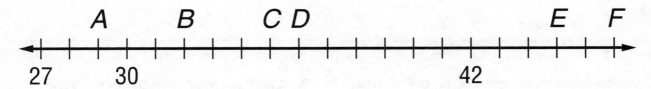

Example:

What number does *D* represent on the number line?

  (A) 34

  (B) 36

  (C) 38

  (D) 40

Answer: (B)

1. **Which letter represents 29 on the number line?**

  (A) A

  (B) B

  (C) C

  (D) D

2. **Which number does *E* represent on the number line?**

  (F) 42

  (G) 43

  (H) 45

  (J) 47

3. **Which letter represents 35 on the number line?**

  (A) B

  (B) C

  (C) D

  (D) E

4. **What number does *B* represent on the number line?**

  (F) 30

  (G) 32

  (H) 34

  (J) 40

GO

Name _____ Date _____

Geometry and Spatial Reasoning

Objective 3

Expectation: *locate and name points on a line using whole numbers*

DIRECTIONS: Use this number line for exercises 5–8.

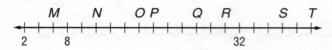

5. Which letter represents 20 on the number line?
   - (A) M
   - (B) N
   - (C) O
   - (D) P

6. Which number does *R* represent on the number line?
   - (F) 25
   - (G) 28
   - (H) 30
   - (J) 32

7. Which of the letter represents 42 on the number line?
   - (A) Q
   - (B) R
   - (C) S
   - (D) T

8. Which two letters would 36 fall between?
   - (F) S and R
   - (G) R and Q
   - (H) Q and P
   - (J) P and O

DIRECTIONS: Use this number line for exercises 9–12.

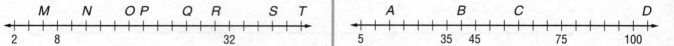

9. Which number represents *A* on the number line?
   - (A) 25
   - (B) 10
   - (C) 20
   - (D) 15

10. Which of the letter represents 60 on the number line?
    - (F) A
    - (G) B
    - (H) C
    - (J) D

11. Which two letters would the midpoint of the number line fall between?
    - (A) A and B
    - (B) B and C
    - (C) C and D
    - (D) None of these

12. Which of the letter represents 105 on the number line?
    - (F) A
    - (G) B
    - (H) C
    - (J) D

STOP

Name _____   Date _____

Objective

| 3 |

Mini-Test

DIRECTIONS: Choose the best answer. Use the number line for exercises 1–2.

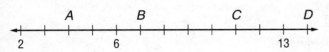

1. Which letter represents 11 on the number line?

Ⓐ A

Ⓑ B

Ⓒ C

Ⓓ D

2. Which number does *D* represent on the number line?

Ⓕ 11

Ⓖ 12

Ⓗ 13

Ⓙ 14

3. Which of the figures below is a sphere?

Ⓐ

Ⓑ

Ⓒ

Ⓓ

4. How many edges does a cube have?

Ⓕ 4

Ⓖ 6

Ⓗ 12

Ⓙ 8

5. The steering wheel on a car is shaped like a _____.

Ⓐ cube

Ⓑ sphere

Ⓒ square

Ⓓ circle

6. How many pairs of congruent figures are on the grid?

Ⓕ 4

Ⓖ 5

Ⓗ 6

Ⓙ 7

STOP

TAKS Mathematics—Objective 4

The student will demonstrate an understanding of the concepts and uses of measurement.

(3.11) Measurement
The student selects and uses appropriate units and procedures to measure length and area. The student is expected to

- **(A)** estimate and measure lengths using standard units such as inch, foot, yard, centimeter, [decimeter,] and meter; *(See page 105.)*
- **(B)** use linear measure to find the perimeter of a shape; and *(See page 107.)*
- **(C)** use [concrete] models of square units to determine the area of shapes. *(See page 109.)*

(3.12) Measurement
The student measures time and temperature. The student is expected to

- **(A)** tell and write time shown on traditional and digital clocks; and *(See page 111.)*
- **(B)** use a thermometer to measure temperature. *(See page 113.)*

(3.13) Measurement
The student applies measurement concepts. The student is expected to

- **(A)** measure to solve problems involving length, [area,] temperature, and time. *(See page 115.)*

Name _____ Date _____

Measurement

Objective 4

Expectation: estimate and measure lengths using standard units such as inch, foot, yard, centimeter, [decimeter,] and meter

DIRECTIONS: Choose the correct answer.

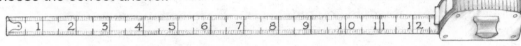

1. **How many inches long is the fish?**

   (A) 5 inches

   (B) 6 inches

   (C) 8 inches

   (D) 12 inches

2. **Look at the paper clip and the pencils. Which pencil is about three inches longer than the paper clip?**

   (F)

   (G)

   (H)

   (J)

3. **Angela wants to measure a piece of wood. Which of these should she use?**

   (A)   (B)   (C)   (D)

GO

Measurement

Objective   **Expectation:** *use linear measure to find the perimeter of a shape*
4

---

4. **If you wanted to measure the length of a football field, what unit would you most likely use?**

    (F)   inches

    (G)   centimeters

    (H)   yards

    (J)   miles

5. **Annette bought a board that is 6 feet long. What is the length of the board in inches?**

    (A)   78 inches

    (B)   72 inches

    (C)   18 inches

    (D)   216 inches

6. **Benjamin is able to kick a soccer ball 33 yards. How many feet is that?**

    (F)   33 feet

    (G)   396 feet

    (H)   99 feet

    (J)   132 feet

7. **The distance between 2 walls is 18 feet. What is the distance in yards?**

    (A)   6 yards

    (B)   3 yards

    (C)   9 yards

    (D)   2 yards

8. **Tonya is 4 feet 11 inches tall. What is her height in inches?**

    (F)   59 inches

    (G)   23 inches

    (H)   44 inches

    (J)   63 inches

9. **A piece of writing paper is 8 1/2 inches by 11 inches. If you wanted to measure a piece of writing paper using the metric system, which unit would you most likely use?**

    (A)   meters

    (B)   centimeters

    (C)   grams

    (D)   liters

10. **Which of these is 1000 meters?**

    (F)   a kilometer

    (G)   0.01 kilometers

    (H)   a centimeter

    (J)   100 centimeters

STOP

Name _____ Date _____

Measurement

Objective
4

Expectation: *use linear measure to find the perimeter of a shape*

 Clue   *Perimeter* is the distance around an area.

DIRECTIONS: Find the perimeter of each figure below. Include the correct units in your answers.

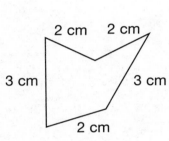

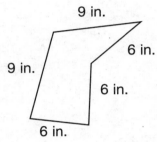

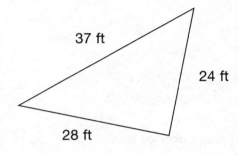

1. _____

2. _____

3. _____

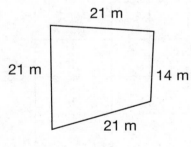

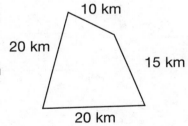

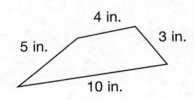

4. _____

5. _____

6. _____

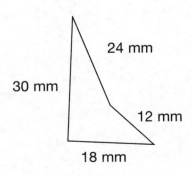

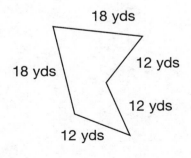

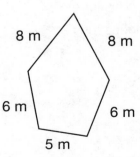

7. _____

8. _____

9. _____

GO

Measurement

Objective
4   ***Expectation:*** *use linear measure to find the perimeter of a shape*

---

10. What is the perimeter of this triangle?

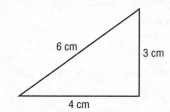

- (A) 13 centimeters
- (B) 12 centimeters
- (C) 17 centimeters
- (D) 18 centimeters

11. If the perimeter of this figure is 50 inches, the missing side is _____.

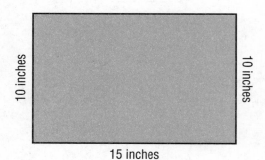

- (F) 15 inches long
- (G) 20 inches long
- (H) 10 inches long
- (J) 25 inches long

12. The perimeter of this figure is _____.

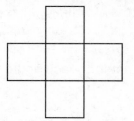

- (A) 12 units
- (B) 20 units
- (C) 14 units
- (D) 4 units

13. What is the perimeter of this figure?

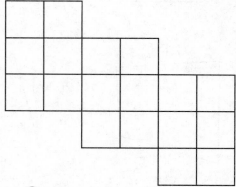

- (F) 22 units
- (G) 14 units
- (H) 18 units
- (J) 24 units

STOP

Name _____ Date _____

Measurement

Objective
4

Expectation: use models of square units to determine the area of shapes

You can estimate the area of an irregular shape by looking at the squares around it. In the example to the right, you know that 4 full squares are covered, so the area will be greater than 4 square units. You also know that the total figure is not larger than 16 square units (4 units × 4 units). You can estimate the area of the figure to be between 4 and 16 square units.

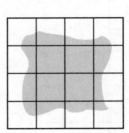

DIRECTIONS: For each of the following figures, estimate the area. Circle the number choice that is most likely the area (in square units) beneath each figure.

1.

3   5   9   2

2.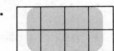

9   8   6   4

3.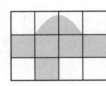

5   6   12   4

DIRECTIONS: *Volume* is the amount of space inside a three-dimensional figure. The volume of 1 cube is 1 cubic unit. Find the number of cubes and volume for each figure below.

4. Number of cubes _____

   Volume = _____ cubic units

5. Number of cubes _____

   Volume = _____ cubic units

6. Number of cubes _____

   Volume = _____ cubic units

GO

Measurement

Objective
4

Expectation: *use models of square units to determine the area of shapes*

---

7. Which of these figures has the largest area.

Ⓐ
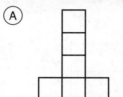

Ⓑ
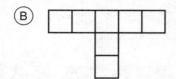

Ⓒ
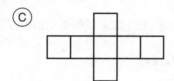

Ⓓ
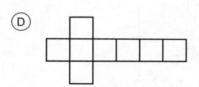

8. Look at the picture of the tile floor. What is the area of the gray tiles?

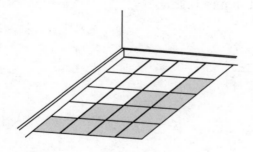

Ⓕ   9 square units

Ⓖ   5 square units

Ⓗ   11 square units

Ⓙ   10 square units

9. What is the area of a square with 4-inch sides?

Ⓐ   12 square inches

Ⓑ   16 square inches

Ⓒ   8 square inches

Ⓓ   32 square inches

10. What is the area of a rectangle that has two sides that are 3 inches long and two sides that are 6 inches long?

Ⓕ   16 square inches

Ⓖ   9 square inches

Ⓗ   36 square inches

Ⓙ   18 square inches

11. If the area of a square is 25 square inches, how long is each side?

Ⓐ   3 inches

Ⓑ   4 inches

Ⓒ   5 inches

Ⓓ   6 inches

STOP

Measurement

Objective 4   **Expectation:** *tell and write time shown on traditional and digital clocks*

DIRECTIONS: Choose the best answer.

Example:

Look at the clock. How long will it take the minute hand to reach the 6?

Ⓐ   3 minutes

Ⓑ   5 minutes

Ⓒ   12 minutes

Ⓓ   15 minutes

Answer: Ⓓ

---

1. **What time is shown on the clock above?**

Ⓐ   2:00

Ⓑ   2:15

Ⓒ   1:15

Ⓓ   3:15

2. **What time is shown on this clock?**

Ⓕ   4:05

Ⓖ   1:40

Ⓗ   1:20

Ⓙ   4:01

3. **What time is shown on this clock?**

Ⓐ   9:50

Ⓑ   9:10

Ⓒ   8:50

Ⓓ   9:45

4. **Which of these clocks shows 5:25?**

Ⓕ

Ⓖ

Ⓗ

Ⓙ

GO

Measurement

Objective 4   *Expectation:* tell and write time shown on traditional and digital clocks

---

5. What time is shown on this clock?

- (A) 1:55
- (B) 2:55
- (C) 11:02
- (D) 11:10

6. Look at the clock below. What time will it be in 40 minutes?

- (F) 6:40
- (G) 7:00
- (H) 7:20
- (J) 7:40

7. What time is shown on this clock?

- (A) 8:20
- (B) 3:40
- (C) 3:08
- (D) 8:40

8. Which clock shows 1:50?

- (F)

- (G)

- (H)

- (J)

9. An alarm clock shows that it is 7:37. Draw this time on the wall clock below.

STOP

Name _____   Date _____

Measurement

Objective
4

Expectation: *use a thermometer to measure temperature*

DIRECTIONS: Choose the best answer.

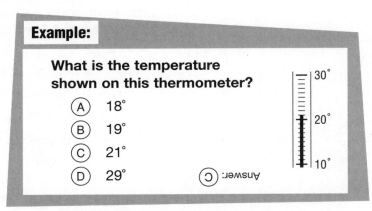

Example:

What is the temperature shown on this thermometer?

Ⓐ 18°
Ⓑ 19°
Ⓒ 21°
Ⓓ 29°

Answer: Ⓒ

1. This thermometer shows the temperature at 8:00 in the morning. By noon, the temperature has risen by 12°. What is the temperature at noon?

Ⓐ 48°
Ⓑ 58°
Ⓒ 60°
Ⓓ 92°

2. What is the temperature shown on the thermometer?

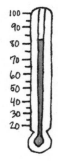

Ⓕ 89°
Ⓖ 66°
Ⓗ 83°
Ⓙ 54°

3. What is the temperature shown on this thermometer?

Ⓐ 9°
Ⓑ 18°
Ⓒ 12°
Ⓓ 10°

4. If today's temperature is between 63.5° and 65.7° degrees, which number below might be the actual temperature?

Ⓕ 64.2°
Ⓖ 66.3°
Ⓗ 63.3°
Ⓙ 62.7°

GO

Measurement

Objective
4

Expectation: *use a thermometer to measure temperature*

DIRECTIONS: Use the thermometers for Saturday and Sunday for exercises 5-7.

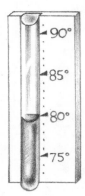

Saturday

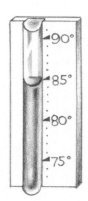

Sunday

5. **What is the temperature shown on the thermometer for Saturday?**

   Ⓐ 75°

   Ⓑ 80°

   Ⓒ 85°

   Ⓓ 90°

6. **Look at the thermometers. How did the temperature change between Saturday and Sunday? On Sunday it was _____ .**

   Ⓕ 5 degrees cooler than on Saturday

   Ⓖ 10 degrees cooler than on Saturday

   Ⓗ 5 degrees warmer than on Saturday

   Ⓙ 10 degrees warmer than on Saturday

7. **What is the temperature shown on the thermometer for Sunday?**

   Ⓐ 75°

   Ⓑ 80°

   Ⓒ 85°

   Ⓓ 90°

STOP

Name _____ Date _____

Measurement

Objective 4

Expectation: measure to solve problems involving length, temperature, and time

DIRECTIONS: Choose the best answer.

1. Rita left dance class at 3:30 p.m. She arrived home at 4:17 p.m. How long did it take Rita to get home?

(A) 1 hour, 17 minutes

(B) 47 minutes

(C) 37 minutes

(D) 13 minutes

2. Look at the sign. If you just missed the 2:10 show, how many minutes will you need to wait for the next one?

AMAZING DOLPHIN SHOW!

Daily at
1:15
2:10
3:05
4:00
4:50

(F) 50 minutes

(G) 45 minutes

(H) 60 minutes

(J) 55 minutes

3. How long is the paperclip?

(A) 3 inches

(B) 5 inches

(C) 3 centimeters

(D) 2 centimeters

4. In the morning, the temperature was 56° F. By noon, the temperature had risen by 9° F. How warm was it at noon?

(F) 60°F

(G) 64°F

(H) 65°F

(J) 70°F

5. On a summer day, you would feel most comfortable at what temperature?

(A) 35°F

(B) 30°F

(C) 95°F

(D) 75°F

GO

Measurement

Objective 4

Expectation: measure to solve problems involving length, temperature, and time

---

6. **Show the time 5:36 on the clock below.**

7. **About how long is this nail?**

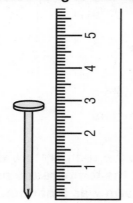

- (F) 1 cm
- (G) 3 cm
- (H) 4 cm
- (J) 6 cm

8. **Which of these statements is true?**

- (A) 1 foot = 21 inches
- (B) 1 foot = 3 inches
- (C) 1 yard = 36 inches
- (D) 1 yard = 39 inches

9. **It takes a train 36 hours to travel from Dallas to Boston. This is the same as _____ .**

- (F) half a day
- (G) a day
- (H) a day and a half
- (J) two days

10. **Jai looked at her watch and saw it was 10:40. Her next class begins in 25 minutes. what time does her next class begin?**

- (A) 10:55
- (B) 11:20
- (C) 11:05
- (D) 10:45

11. **Which unit of measurement is longer than a foot but shorter than a meter?**

- (F) a yard
- (G) a meter
- (H) a centimeter
- (J) a mile

STOP

Objective

4

Mini-Test

DIRECTIONS: Choose the best answer.

1. What is the perimeter of the polygon?

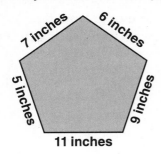

- (A) 38 inches
- (B) 26 inches
- (C) 28 inches
- (D) 29 inches

2. If the perimeter of this figure is 88 inches, the missing side is _____ .

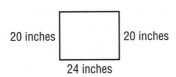

- (F) 12 inches
- (G) 20 inches
- (H) 24 inches
- (J) 44 inches

3. What is the area of this figure?

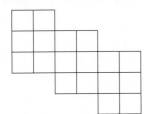

- (A) 22 units
- (B) 14 units
- (C) 16 units
- (D) 18 units

4. Look at the shaded area in this picture. If each square is an inch, what is the area of the shaded part?

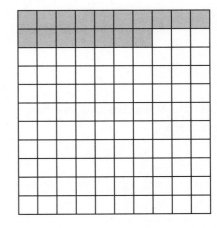

- (F) 289 square inches
- (G) 150 square inches
- (H) 19 square inches
- (J) 17 square inches

5. What time does the clock show?

- (A) 9:45
- (B) 10:15
- (C) 10:45
- (D) 11:00

GO

6. What time does the clock show?

   (F)   7:30

   (G)   7:20

   (H)   7:25

   (J)   7:35

7. What is the temperature on the thermometer?

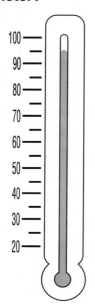

   (A)   87°F

   (B)   95°F

   (C)   100°F

   (D)   90°F

8. In the morning, the temperature was 56°F. By noon, the temperature had risen by 9°F. How warm was it at noon?

   (F)   60°F

   (G)   64°F

   (H)   65°F

   (J)   70°F

9. A lamp that is 23 inches tall is _____.

   (A)   less than 2 feet tall

   (B)   more than 2 feet tall

   (C)   less than 1 foot tall

   (D)   equal to 2 feet in height

10. Look at the clock. How long will it take for the minute hand to reach the 9?

   (F)   3 minutes

   (G)   30 minutes

   (H)   5 minutes

   (J)   15 minutes

11. Sara wants to make a flag for her class project. The flag has to be 24 inches long and 12 inches wide. How many square feet of fabric will she need?

   (A)   1

   (B)   2

   (C)   3

   (D)   4

STOP

TAKS Mathematics—Objective 5

The student will demonstrate an understanding of probability and statistics.

(3.14) Probability and statistics
The student solves problems by collecting, organizing, displaying, and interpreting sets of data. The student is expected to

(A) [collect,] organize, record, and display data in pictographs and bar graphs where each picture or cell might represent more than one piece of data; *(See page 120.)*

What it means:
- A *pictograph* is a graph that uses pictures instead of numbers to represent a number of people or things.

(B) interpret information from pictographs and bar graphs; and *(See page 122.)*

(C) use data to describe events as more likely, less likely, or equally likely. *(See page 124.)*

Probability and Statistics

Objective 5

Expectation: *organize, record, and display data in pictographs and bar graphs where each picture or cell might represent more than one piece of data*

Roll	1	2	3	4	5	6	7	8	9	10	11	12	13	14	15	16	17	18	19	20
Number Rolled	3	6	1	4	6	1	5	3	3	6	4	2	6	5	3	1	4	4	3	6

DIRECTIONS: A student rolled a 6-sided number cube 20 times. The results are shown in the table above. Read the table and use the information to fill in the line graph. Then answer the questions.

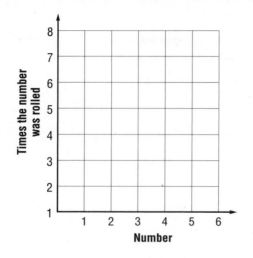

1. **How many times did the student roll a 4?**
   - (A) 2
   - (B) 3
   - (C) 4
   - (D) 5

2. **What number did he roll the least?**
   - (F) 1
   - (G) 2
   - (H) 3
   - (J) 6

3. **How many times did he roll an even number?**
   - (A) 10
   - (B) 12
   - (C) 13
   - (D) 14

4. **How many times did he roll an odd number?**
   - (F) 13
   - (G) 14
   - (H) 10
   - (J) 16

5. **What two numbers came up the most?**
   - (A) 2, 5
   - (B) 1, 2
   - (C) 1, 5
   - (D) 3, 6

GO

Probability and Statistics

Objective 5

Expectation: *organize, record, and display data in pictographs and bar graphs where each picture or cell might represent more than one piece of data*

---

6. **Use this information to make a bar graph in the space below.**

June $4\frac{1}{2}$ inches

July $3\frac{1}{2}$ inches

August   2 inches

7. **Draw a picture graph that shows how many boys and girls are in your class at school. Use a picture of one girl for every five girls in your class. Use a picture of one boy for every five boys in your class.**

STOP

Probability and Statistics

Objective
5

Expectation: interpret information from pictographs and bar graphs

DIRECTIONS: The third grade students at Millbrook School made a graph about where they wanted to go on vacation. Study the graph, then answer questions 1–4.

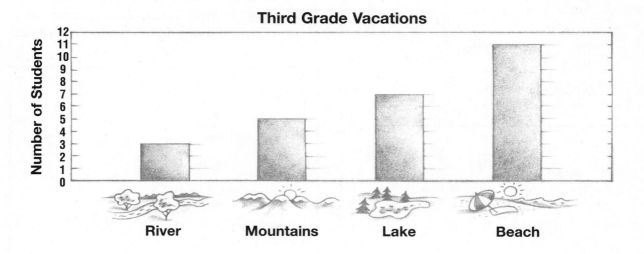

Third Grade Vacations

1. **Which of these is another way to show how many students went to the beach?**

   Ⓐ ☓☓☓☓ ☓☓☓☓ |
   Ⓑ ☓☓☓☓ |
   Ⓒ ☓☓☓☓ ☓☓☓☓
   Ⓓ ☓☓☓☓ ☓☓☓☓ ||/|

2. **Two of the students changed their minds and decided to go to a lake instead of the beach. How many students then wanted to go to a lake?**

   Ⓕ 7
   Ⓖ 8
   Ⓗ 5
   Ⓙ 9

3. **How many students went to a lake for vacation?**

   Ⓐ 11
   Ⓑ 7
   Ⓒ 8
   Ⓓ 5

4. **What was the third graders favorite vacation spot?**

   Ⓕ river
   Ⓖ mountains
   Ⓗ lake
   Ⓙ beach

GO

Probability and Statistics

Objective
5

Expectation: interpret information from pictographs and bar graphs

---

5. **Look at the graph below and the report Willie made about the coins in his change jar. How many dimes did Willie have in the change jar?**

(A) 7
(B) 11
(C) 18
(D) 6

> **Willie's Report**
> I had more pennies than any other coin. Nickels were the fewest. I had more dimes than quarters.

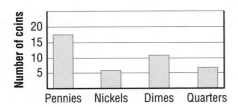

6. **Which animal is between 15 and 40 feet long?**

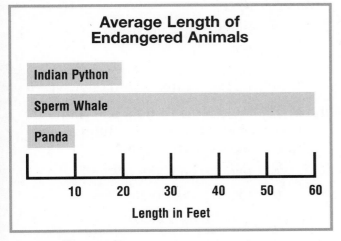

(F) panda
(G) sperm whale
(H) Indian python
(J) not here

7. **In a pictograph** **stands for 5 books.**

How many books does

stand for?

(A) 5 books
(B) 8 books
(C) 20 books
(D) 40 books

8. **How much did the average daily temperature change from February to March?**

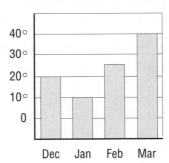

(F) 25°F
(G) 15°F
(H) 10°F
(J) 5°F

STOP

Name _____   Date _____

Probability and Statistics

Objective 5

Expectation: *use data to describe events as more likely, less likely, or equally likely*

 Clue   Review the numbers and colors of each button as you read the answers.

DIRECTIONS: Choose the best answer.

Melanie put 3 yellow buttons, 6 red buttons, 2 blue buttons, and 1 green button in a bag. Mikel draws one button out of the bag each time. Answer the questions below.

1. **What is the chance that Mikel will pull out a yellow button?**
   - (A) 3 out of 12
   - (B) 4 out of 12
   - (C) 1 out of 12
   - (D) 6 out of 12

2. **What is the chance that Mikel will pull out a blue button?**
   - (F) 1 out of 12
   - (G) 4 out of 12
   - (H) 5 out of 12
   - (J) 2 out of 12

3. **What is the chance that Mikel will pull out a red button?**
   - (A) 4 out of 12
   - (B) 6 out of 12
   - (C) 3 out of 12
   - (D) 2 out of 12

4. **What is the chance that Mikel will pull out a green button?**
   - (F) 2 out of 12
   - (G) 4 out of 12
   - (H) 1 out of 12
   - (J) 6 out of 12

5. **Which color is Mikel most likely to pull out?**
   - (A) yellow
   - (B) blue
   - (C) red
   - (D) green

6. **Which color is Mikel least likely to pull out?**
   - (F) yellow
   - (G) blue
   - (H) red
   - (J) green

7. **What should Melanie do if she wants to have an equal chance of getting a blue button and a green button?**
   - (A) add 1 green button
   - (B) remove 1 red button
   - (C) add 1 blue button
   - (D) remove 1 green button

GO

Name _____ Date _____

Probability and Statistics

Objective 5

Expectation: use data to describe events as more likely, less likely, or equally likely

DIRECTIONS: Use the spinner to answer the questions.

Spinner 1   **Spinner 2**

8. **How many different objects are on Spinner 1?**
   - (F) 1
   - (G) 2
   - (H) 3
   - (J) 4

9. **What are the chances of spinning a square on Spinner 1?**
   - (A) 0 out of 4
   - (B) 1 out of 4
   - (C) 2 out of 4
   - (D) 3 out of 4

10. **What are the chances of spinning a circle on Spinner 1?**
   - (F) 1 out of 4
   - (G) 2 out of 4
   - (H) 3 out of 4
   - (J) 4 out of 4

11. **How many different objects are on Spinner 2?**
   - (A) 2
   - (B) 4
   - (C) 6
   - (D) 8

12. **How many sections are there on Spinner 2?**
   - (F) 2
   - (G) 4
   - (H) 6
   - (J) 8

13. **How many stars are on Spinner 2?**
   - (A) 2
   - (B) 3
   - (C) 4
   - (D) 1

14. **What are the chances of spinning a star on Spinner 2?**
   - (F) 3 out of 4
   - (G) 2 out of 8
   - (H) 3 out of 4
   - (J) 3 out of 8

15. **What are the chances of spinning a square on Spinner 2?**
   - (A) 2 out of 8
   - (B) 3 out of 8
   - (C) 1 out of 8
   - (D) 4 out of 8

16. **Which object are you least likely to spin on Spinner 2?**
   - (F) circle
   - (G) star
   - (H) triangle
   - (J) square

STOP

Objective

5

Mini-Test

DIRECTIONS: use the charts and information in the questions to answer numbers 1-9.

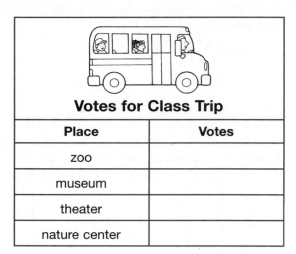

Votes for Class Trip

Place	Votes
zoo	
museum	
theater	
nature center	

Key
= 6 students
= 3 students

1. **If 12 students voted to go to the zoo, how many 👤 would be in the pictograph?**

   - Ⓐ 1.5
   - Ⓑ 2
   - Ⓒ 2.5
   - Ⓓ 3.5

2. **If 21 students voted for the museum, how many 👤 would be in the pictograph?**

   - Ⓕ 1.5
   - Ⓖ 2
   - Ⓗ 2.5
   - Ⓙ 3.5

3. **If 9 students voted for the theater, how many 👤 would be in the pictograph?**

   - Ⓐ 1.5
   - Ⓑ 2
   - Ⓒ 2.5
   - Ⓓ 3.5

4. **If 15 students voted for the nature center, how many 👤 would be in the pictograph?**

   - Ⓕ 1.5
   - Ⓖ 2
   - Ⓗ 2.5
   - Ⓙ 3.5

5. **Use questions 1–4 to find the total number of students who voted.**

   - Ⓐ 9.5
   - Ⓑ 57
   - Ⓒ 11
   - Ⓓ 66

6. **How many more students voted for the zoo than for the theater?**

   - Ⓕ 3
   - Ⓖ 12
   - Ⓗ 6
   - Ⓙ 9

GO

7. Which place received the most votes?

(A) Zoo

(B) Museum

(C) Theater

(D) Nature Center

8. Which place received the least votes?

(F) Zoo

(G) Museum

(H) Theater

(J) Nature Center

9. Twelve students were absent the day of the vote. If 6 of them voted for the museum, and 6 of them voted for the theater, would that change the winning vote for the class trip?

(A) No, the Museum still wins.

(B) Yes, the Zoo will win.

(C) Yes, the Theater will win.

(D) No, the Nature Center still wins.

DIRECTIONS: Use the following information for exercises 10–11. Marlow noticed that the parking lot at the store had 11 red cars, 6 blue cars, 4 white cars, and 3 cars of other colors.

10. If someone leaves the building and walks to a car, which color car is it most likely to be?

(F) red

(G) blue

(H) white

(J) another color

11. If someone leaves the building and walks to a car, which color car is it least likely to be?

(A) red

(B) blue

(C) white

(D) another color

DIRECTIONS: Choose the best answer.

12. The children in the Adams family were stuck inside on a rainy day. They decided to make their own games. They each made a spinner. When Jennie spun her spinner, the color it landed on was gray. Which spinner was probably Jennie's?

(F)
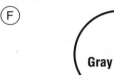

(G)
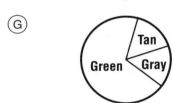

(H)
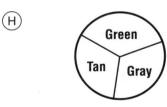

(J)

STOP

TAKS Mathematics—Objective 6

The student will demonstrate an understanding of the mathematical processes and tools used in problem solving.

(3.15) Underlying processes and mathematical tools.
The student applies Grade 3 mathematics to solve problems connected to everyday experiences and activities in and outside of school. The student is expected to
- **(A)** identify the mathematics in everyday situations; *(See page 129.)*
- **(B)** use a problem-solving model that incorporates understanding the problem, making a plan, carrying out the plan, and evaluating the solution for reasonableness; and *(See page 131.)*
- **(C)** select or develop an appropriate problem-solving strategy, including drawing a picture, looking for a pattern, systematic guessing and checking, acting it out, making a table, working a simpler problem, or working backwards to solve a problem. *(See page 133.)*

(3.16) Underlying processes and mathematical tools
The student communicates about Grade 3 mathematics using informal language. The student is expected to
- **(B)** relate informal language to mathematical language and symbols. *(See page 135.)*

What it means:

- Relating informal language to mathematical language and symbols means that students will be able to turn a word problem into a mathematical situation. For example, students should understand that the words "less than" indicate that they will need to subtract.

(3.17) Underlying processes and mathematical tools
The student uses logical reasoning to make sense of his or her world. The student is expected to
- **(A)** make generalizations from patterns or sets of examples and nonexamples. *(See page 137.)*

Underlying Processes and Mathematical Tools

Objective
6

Expectation: *identify the mathematics in everyday situations*

DIRECTIONS: Janna's favorite cereal cost $3.00 when she was 6 years old. It cost $3.50 when she was 8 years old, $4.00 when she was 9, and $4.50 when she was 10. Use the table to answer the questions.

Price of Cereal	
Year	Cost
1	$3.00
2	$3.50
3	$4.00
4	$4.50

1. In what year was the price the lowest?

(A) 1

(B) 2

(C) 3

(D) 4

2. How much did the price of cereal change over 4 years?

(F) $.50

(G) $1.00

(H) $1.50

(J) $2.00

3. What happened to the price of cereal between year 1 and year 4?

(A) it doubled

(B) it went up

(C) it stayed the same

(D) it went down

4. Predict what you think a box of cereal will cost in year 5.

(F) $5.50

(G) $3.00

(H) $4.50

(J) $5.00

5. Which graph correctly shows the change in price of Janna's cereal?

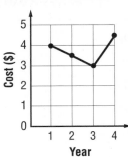

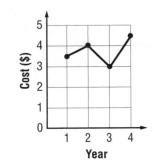

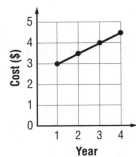

(D) None of these

GO

Underlying Processes and Mathematical Tools

Objective 6

Expectation: *identify the mathematics in everyday situations*

---

6. A box of popcorn costs $1.25. You pay for it with two dollar bills. How much change will you receive?

   F) $2.00 ÷ $1.25 = ■
   G) $1.25 + $2.00 = ■
   H) $2.00 × $1.25 = ■
   J) $2.00 − $1.25 = ■

7. A plane has 124 passengers. There are 3 members of the flying crew and 9 cabin attendants. How many people are on the plane?

   A) 136
   B) 135
   C) 133
   D) 112

8. Mr. Hoy planted 45 seeds in the fall. He planted 20 tomato seeds, 15 cucumber seeds, and the rest were onion seeds. How many onion seeds were there?

   F) 15
   G) 12
   H) 10
   J) 5

9. Connor saves $3.25 of his allowance every month and puts it in the bank. How much will he have saved in one year?

   A) $32.50
   B) $39.00
   C) $36.25
   D) $36.00

10. The owner of a car factory wants to buy enough tires to use on 143 cars. How many tires will the owner need to buy?

    F) 143
    G) 572
    H) 366
    J) 286

11. Rachel's recipe calls for three pints of milk. There are two cups in one pint. How would Rachel find out how many cups of milk she needs for her recipe?

    A) 3 × 1 = 3
    B) 3 × 2 = 6
    C) 3 ÷ 1 = 3
    D) 3 + 2 = 5

12. Sara has to finish her drawing for art class. She can work on it Saturday morning between 8 and 10:30. She begins at 8 but doesn't finish until 11:15. How many minutes did she work past 10:30?

    F) 20
    G) 30
    H) 45
    J) 50

13. Which combination of coins makes $.82?

    A) 2 quarters, 3 dimes, 1 nickel
    B) 4 quarters and 2 pennies
    C) 3 quarters, 1 nickel, and 2 pennies
    D) 1 quarter, 3 dimes, 1 nickel, and 2 pennies

STOP

Underlying Processes and Mathematical Tools

Objective 6

Expectation: use a problem-solving model that incorporates understanding the problem, making a plan, carrying out the plan, and evaluating the solution for reasonableness

 Clue Break each problem into parts to help you understand it.

DIRECTIONS: Choose the best answer.

1. Jennie had three bent nails in her pocket. Then she put five straight nails in her pocket. Which answer shows what she had in her pocket?

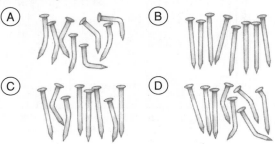

(A)   (B)

(C)   (D)

2. Tai carried 4 boxes of tiles into the kitchen. Each box held 12 tiles. What would you do to find out how many tiles he carried into the kitchen all together?

(F) multiply

(G) subtract

(H) divide

(J) None of these

3. Which of these is most likely measured in feet?

(A) the distance around a room

(B) the weight of a large box

(C) the distance to the moon

(D) the amount of water in a pool

4. This map shows Janelle's yard. She came in through the gate and walked east for 3 yards. Then she went north for 2 yards. What was she closest to?

(F) the swing

(G) the pond

(H) the steps

(J) the garden

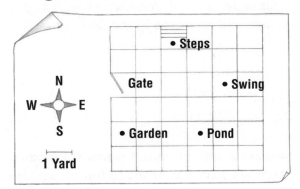

5. Rick is carving a pattern in a piece of wood. Which shapes are missing from the pattern?

(A)   (B)   (C)   (D)

GO

Underlying Processes and Mathematical Tools

Objective 6

Expectation: use a problem-solving model that incorporates understanding the problem, making a plan, carrying out the plan, and evaluating the solution for reasonableness

6. **Michael has 4 quarters and 2 dimes for bus fare. If the bus ride costs $.75, how much money will he have left?**

(F) $.25

(G) $.35

(H) $.45

(J) $.50

7. **Cody played in 3 basketball games. In the first game, he scored 17 points. In the second game, he scored 22 points. In the third game, he scored twice as many points as in his first game. How many points did he score in the third game?**

(A) 44 points

(B) 36 points

(C) 34 points

(D) 42 points

8. **A worker at Command Software makes $720 a week. You want to figure out how much he makes an hour. What other piece of information do you need?**

(F) the number of weeks the worker works each year

(G) the number of vacation days the worker takes

(H) how much money the worker makes each day

(J) how many hours a day the worker works

DIRECTIONS: Use the graph to answer questions 9–10.

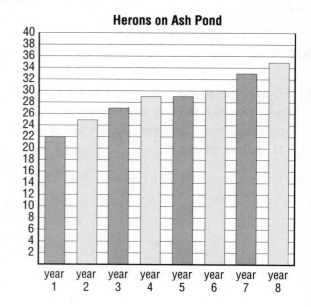

Herons on Ash Pond

9. **In which two years did the number of herons stay the same?**

(A) years 1 and 2

(B) years 2 and 3

(C) years 3 and 4

(D) years 4 and 5

10. **How many more herons were there in year 8 than in year 1?**

(F) 10

(G) 11

(H) 13

(J) 14

STOP

Name _____   Date _____

Underlying Processes and Mathematical Tools

Objective 6

Expectation: select or develop an appropriate problem-solving strategy, including drawing a picture, looking for a pattern, systematic guessing and checking, acting it out, making a table, working a simpler problem, or working backwards to solve a problem

---

Example:

Which number sentence shows the total number of beans?

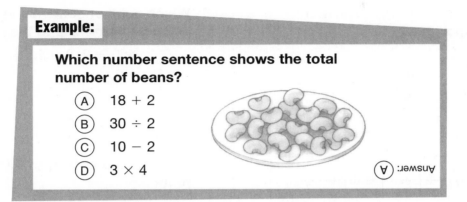

Ⓐ   18 + 2
Ⓑ   30 ÷ 2
Ⓒ   10 − 2
Ⓓ   3 × 4

Answer: (A)

Clue   Decide what useful information you can get from a picture, chart, or graph before you read the question.

---

1. **Sarah just read that her town has the highest population in the county. Based on the chart below, in which city does Sarah live?**

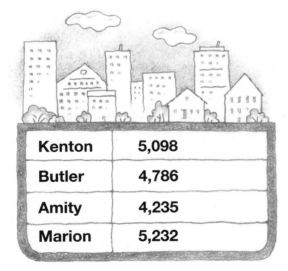

Kenton	5,098
Butler	4,786
Amity	4,235
Marion	5,232

Ⓐ   Kenton
Ⓑ   Butler
Ⓒ   Amity
Ⓓ   Marion

2. **Look at the pattern of fruit. Which of these is the missing piece of fruit?**

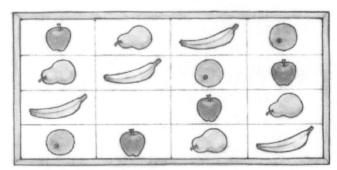

Ⓕ   orange
Ⓖ   banana
Ⓗ   pear
Ⓙ   apple

GO

Underlying Processes and Mathematical Tools

Objective 6

Expectation: *select or develop an appropriate problem-solving strategy, including drawing a picture, looking for a pattern, systematic guessing and checking, acting it out, making a table, working a simpler problem, or working backwards to solve a problem*

DIRECTIONS: Use this calendar to answer questions 3 through 5.

January						
SUN	**MON**	**TUE**	**WED**	**THU**	**FRI**	**SAT**
1	2	3	4	5	6	7
8	9	10	11	12	13	14
15	16	17	18	19	20	21
22	23	24	25	26	27	28
29	30	31				

3. **This calendar is for January. What day of the week was the last day in December?**
   - (A) Monday
   - (B) Saturday
   - (C) Sunday
   - (D) Tuesday

4. **How many Tuesdays are in January?**
   - (F) 3
   - (G) 4
   - (H) 5
   - (J) 6

5. **For the class trip this year, the students are going on a camping trip. The trip will begin on the third Wednesday in January and ending the following Saturday. What date will the camping trip begin?**
   - (A) January 4
   - (B) January 25
   - (C) January 21
   - (D) January 18

6. **Which number sentence would you use to estimate 448 ÷ 212 to the nearest 100?**
   - (F) 450 ÷ 210
   - (G) 440 ÷ 210
   - (H) 500 ÷ 200
   - (J) 400 ÷ 200

7. **Estimate the answer to this problem by rounding.**

   56 × 12
   - (A) 500
   - (B) 600
   - (C) 560
   - (D) 1,000

8. **Which of these should you use to estimate 44 − 19 to the nearest 10?**
   - (F) 40 − 20
   - (G) 45 − 15
   - (H) 50 − 20
   - (J) 40 − 10

9. **Which of these would you probably measure in meters?**
   - (A) the height of a tree
   - (B) the distance between two cities
   - (C) the weight of a horse
   - (D) the amount of medicine in a bottle

STOP

Name _____   Date _____

Underlying Processes and Mathematical Tools

Objective 6

Expectation: *relate informal language to mathematical language and symbols*

Example:

18 ■ 9 = 9

Which operation sign belongs in the box above?

(A) +

(B) −

(C) ×

(D) ÷

Answer: (B)

 Clue

When you are not sure of an answer, make your best guess and move on to the next problem.

DIRECTIONS: Choose the best answer.

1. Which operation sign belongs in both boxes?

27 ■ 8 = 19   10 ■ 2 = 8

(A) +

(B) −

(C) ×

(D) ÷

2. You have a bag of candy to share with your class. There are 25 students in your class. You want each student to get 7 pieces. What operation will you need to use to figure out how many candies you need?

(F) addition

(G) subtraction

(H) multiplication

(J) division

3. Look at the figure. What is its perimeter?

(A) 20 inches

(B) 15 inches

(C) 12 inches

(D) 38 inches

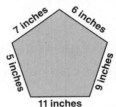

7 inches   6 inches
5 inches   9 inches
11 inches

4. Tad wants to find the weight of a box of cereal. What unit of measurement will he probably find on the side of the box?

(F) millimeters

(G) pounds

(H) hectoliters

(J) ounces

GO

Underlying Processes and Mathematical Tools

Objective 6

Expectation: relate informal language to mathematical language and symbols

5. Which of these numbers shows 587 rounded to the nearest hundred?

(A) 580

(B) 500

(C) 690

(D) 600

6. How can you write 9,876 in expanded notation?

(F) 9,800 + 76 + 0

(G) 9,800 + 70 + 60

(H) 9,000 + 870 + 60

(J) 9,000 + 800 + 70 + 6

7. Which of these numbers has a 1 in the tens place and a 7 in the ones place?

(A) 710

(B) 701

(C) 517

(D) 471

8. What sign correctly completes the number sentence?

24 ■ 6 = 4

(F) ÷

(G) −

(H) +

(J) ×

9. What sign correctly completes the number sentence?

72 ■ 9 = 63

(A) ÷

(B) −

(C) +

(D) ×

10. Which decimal is equal to $\frac{1}{4}$?

(F) 0.25

(G) 0.025

(H) 0.75

(J) .033

11.

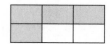

From the figure above, you know that _____.

(A) $\frac{4}{3}$ is greater than $\frac{2}{3}$

(B) $\frac{2}{8}$ is greater than $\frac{4}{8}$

(C) $\frac{2}{6}$ is greater than $\frac{4}{6}$

(D) $\frac{4}{6}$ is greater than $\frac{2}{6}$

12. Which amount is the same as 25 cents?

(F) $\frac{1}{4}$ dollar

(G) $\frac{1}{2}$ dollar

(H) $\frac{2}{3}$ dollar

(J) $\frac{3}{4}$ dollar

STOP

Name _____ Date _____

Underlying Processes and Mathematical Tools

Objective 6

Expectation: make generalizations from patterns or sets of examples and nonexamples

 Clue Use scratch paper to help you remember steps and numbers in each problem.

DIRECTIONS: Choose the best answer.

1. **What letter is missing from this pattern?**

    C D E _____ G C D E F G

    (A) C

    (B) A

    (C) G

    (D) F

2. **Michael was at a card convention. At the first booth he bought 8 cards. He bought 6 cards at each of the remaining 9 booths. How many cards did Michael buy altogether?**

    (F) 54 cards

    (G) 62 cards

    (H) 57 cards

    (J) 72 cards

3. **There were 85 boxes shipped to the warehouse. In each box there were 22 cartons. In each carton there were 40 water guns. How many water guns are in all 85 boxes?**

    (A) 880

    (B) 1,870

    (C) 74,800

    (D) Not enough information

4. **A total of 60 people brought their pets to a pet show. Half the people brought dogs and 20 people brought cats. How many people brought other kinds of pets?**

    (F) 30

    (G) 10

    (H) 20

    (J) 40

5. **A doctor has her office open 5 days a week, 8 hours a day. If she sees 4 patients an hour, how many patients does she see in 1 day?**

    (A) 24

    (B) 28

    (C) 38

    (D) 32

6. **What number is missing from this pattern?**

    7, 11, 15, _____, 23

    (F) 19

    (G) 12

    (H) 16

    (J) 14

GO

Underlying Processes and Mathematical Tools

Objective 6

Expectation: *make generalizations from patterns or sets of examples and non-examples*

DIRECTIONS: Some numbers are missing from the chart below. Look for patterns and then fill in the chart before you answer the questions.

 Clue Which operation is this table based on (+, −, x, ÷)?

1		3			6			9	10
2	4			10			16		20
3			12			21			30
4		12			24			36	40
5	10			25			40		50
6			24			42			60
7		21			42			63	70
8	16			40			64		80
9			36			63			90
10		30			60				100

1. **Circle all the odd numbers.**
   How many squares have circles? _____

2. **Put an X over the following number patterns when you find them in the grid:**
   20, 27, 32, 35, 36, 35, 32, 27, 20
   5, 8, 9, 8, 5
   8, 14, 18, 20, 20, 18, 14, 8
   50, 54, 56, 56, 54, 50

3. **How many squares have both a circle and an X?** _____

STOP

Objective

6

Mini-Test

DIRECTIONS: Choose the best answer.

1. **Mr. Lowell paid $0.59 for a bag of chips and $0.39 for a bottle of juice. How much money did he spend all together?**

   Ⓐ $0.79

   Ⓑ $0.88

   Ⓒ $0.89

   Ⓓ $0.98

2. **Which two things together would cost about $30.00?**

   Ⓕ hat and shirt

   Ⓖ belt and socks

   Ⓗ shirt and socks

   Ⓙ hat and belt

$25.00

$4.50

$18.00

$15.00

3. **The following is a list of how many baseball cards these friends collected: Tanya—207, Mercedes—287, Jared— 278, and Lance—239. Which of the following answers shows the baseball card collections arranged from least cards to most?**

   Ⓐ Tanya, Lance, Mercedes, Jared

   Ⓑ Tanya, Lance, Jared, Mercedes

   Ⓒ Lance, Tanya, Mercedes, Jared

   Ⓓ Mercedes, Jared, Lance, Tanya

4. **Leah is making an orange punch recipe in a very large punch bowl. Orange juice comes in different-sized containers. Which sized container should she buy in order to purchase the fewest number of containers?**

   Ⓕ A one-cup container

   Ⓖ A one-gallon container

   Ⓗ A one-pint container

   Ⓙ A one-quart container

5. **Shawn is collecting stones for a project. On the first day, he collects 100. On the second day, he collects 20. On the third, he finds 3 stones. Which number shows how many stones he collected in all?**

   Ⓐ 23

   Ⓑ 123

   Ⓒ 1,023

   Ⓓ 24

6. **Colleen found 16 shells on Saturday and 17 shells on Sunday. Al found 12 shells on Saturday and 22 shells on Sunday. Who found the greater number of shells all together?**

   Ⓕ Al

   Ⓖ Colleen

   Ⓗ They found the same number of shells.

   Ⓙ Not enough information

STOP

How Am I Doing?

Objective 1 Mini-Test Page 81 **Number Correct**	**7–8** answers correct	**Great Job!** Move on to the section test on page 142.
	5–6 answers correct	**You're almost there!** But you still need a little practice. Review practice pages 59–80 before moving on to the section test on page 142.
	0–4 answers correct	**Oops!** Time to review what you have learned and try again. Review the practice section on pages 59–80. Then retake the test on page 81. Now move on to the section test on page 142.
Objective 2 Mini-Test Page 93 **Number Correct**	**6** answers correct	**Awesome!** Move on to the section test on page 142.
	4–5 answers correct	**You're almost there!** But you still need a little practice. Review practice pages 83–92 before moving on to the section test on page 142.
	0–3 answers correct	**Oops!** Time to review what you have learned and try again. Review the practice section on pages 83–92. Then retake the test on page 93. Now move on to the section test on page 142.
Objective 3 Mini-Test Page 103 **Number Correct**	**6** answers correct	**Great Job!** Move on to the section test on page 142.
	4–5 answers correct	**You're almost there!** But you still need a little practice. Review practice pages 95–102 before moving on to the section test on page 142.
	0–3 answers correct	**Oops!** Time to review what you have learned and try again. Review the practice section on pages 95–102. Then retake the test on page 103. Now move on to the section test on page 142.

How Am I Doing?

Objective 4 Mini-Test	**5** answers correct	**Great Job!** Move on to the section test on page 142.
	3–4 answers correct	**You're almost there!** But you still need a little practice. Review practice pages 105–116 before moving on to the section test on page 142.
Page 117 **Number Correct**	**0–2** answers correct	**Oops!** Time to review what you have learned and try again. Review the practice section on pages 105–116. Then retake the test on page 117. Now move on to the section test on page 142.
Objective 5 Mini-Test	**6** answers correct	**Awesome!** Move on to the section test on page 142.
	4–5 answers correct	**You're almost there!** But you still need a little practice. Review practice pages 120–125 before moving on to the section test on page 142.
Page 126 **Number Correct**	**0–3** answers correct	**Oops!** Time to review what you have learned and try again. Review the practice section on pages 120–125. Then retake the test on page 126. Now move on to the section test on page 142.
Objective 6 Mini-Test	**6** answers correct	**Great Job!** Move on to the section test on page 142.
	4–5 answers correct	**You're almost there!** But you still need a little practice. Review practice pages 129–138 before moving on to the section test on page 142.
Page 139 **Number Correct**	**0–3** answers correct	**Oops!** Time to review what you have learned and try again. Review the practice section on pages 129–138. Then retake the test on page 139. Now move on to the section test on page 142.

Final Mathematics Test
for pages 60–139

DIRECTIONS: Choose the best answer.

1. **What is the meaning of 1,976?**

   Ⓐ one thousand nine hundred seventy-six

   Ⓑ one hundred ninety-six

   Ⓒ nineteen thousand seventy-six

   Ⓓ nineteen seventy-sixes

2. **Lillian rode her bicycle to the supermarket for her mother. Here is the change she was given when she bought one of the items on the table with a five-dollar bill. Which item did she buy?**

   Ⓕ  $3.65

   Ⓖ  $4.55

   Ⓗ  $3.50

   Ⓙ  $4.79

3. **Which of these figures is $\frac{4}{7}$ shaded?**

   Ⓐ

   Ⓑ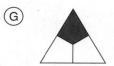

   Ⓒ

   Ⓓ

4. **What picture shows a fraction equivalent to $\frac{3}{10}$?**

   Ⓕ

   Ⓖ

   Ⓗ

   Ⓙ

GO

5. **Which number sentence shows how to find the total number of feathers?**

- (A) 3 + 4
- (B) 3 ÷ 4
- (C) 4 − 3
- (D) 4 × 3

6. **27 ● 8 = 19   10 ● 2 = 8**
Which operation sign belongs in both boxes above?

- (F) +
- (G) −
- (H) ×
- (J) ÷

7. **210 × 5 =**

- (A) 1,050
- (B) 1,500
- (C) 1,005
- (D) Not Here

8. **Which number is an even number and can be divided evenly by 7?**

- (F) 26
- (G) 35
- (H) 14
- (J) 60

9. **Round these numbers to the nearest hundred: 179, 245, 212, 191, 255, 149. How many of them will be 200?**

- (A) 3
- (B) 4
- (C) 5
- (D) 6

10. **Which number sentence would you use to estimate 97 × 9 to the nearest 100?**

- (F) 90 × 5
- (G) 100 × 10
- (H) 90 × 10
- (J) 100 × 5

11. **After school, Brian has 3 hours before dinnertime. If he spends an hour and fifteen minutes playing his drums, how much time is left to do his homework and play with his friends before dinner?**

- (A) more than 2 hours
- (B) less than 2 hours
- (C) 2 1/2 hours
- (D) 3 hours

12. **Which number sentence shows how to find the total number of butterflies?**

- (F) 2 + 4
- (G) 4 ÷ 2
- (H) 4 − 2
- (J) 2 × 4

GO

13. Yoshi used this clue to find the secret number to open the briefcase. What is the secret number?

If you double the secret number and then add 4, the answer is 20.

(A) 12
(B) 10
(C) 8
(D) 6

DIRECTIONS: A parking attendant uses the table to keep track of his income. Use this table for questions 14–15.

Number of Cars	Amount
1	$5
2	$10
3	●

14. How much does parking cost per car?

(F) $3
(G) $5
(H) $10
(J) $15

15. What number will replace the ●?

(A) $3
(B) $5
(C) $10
(D) $15

16. Kim made one straight cut across the trapezoid. Which pair of figures could be the two cut pieces of the trapezoid?

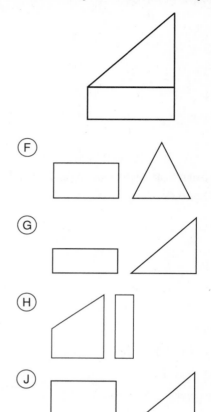

(F)

(G)

(H)

(J)

17. Which of the following shapes is not congruent to the others?

(A)

(B)

(C)

(D)

GO

Name _____   Date _____

18. Which letter has a line of symmetry?

(F) **J**

(G) **S**

(H) **M**

(J) **Q**

19. What number does the *A* on the number line represent?

(A) 14

(B) 10

(C) 7

(D) 3

20. Which of these paper clips is approximately 2 inches long?

(F)

(G)

(H)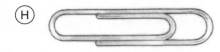

(J)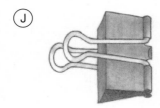

21. What is the perimeter of the rectangle?

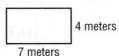

4 meters

7 meters

(A) 22 meters

(B) 18 meters

(C) 11 meters

(D) 3 meters

22. What is the area of the shaded region?

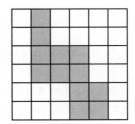

(F) 36

(G) 20

(H) 12

(J) 24

23. What time is shown on the clock?

(A) 8:07

(B) 8:35

(C) 7:35

(D) 7:40

GO

145

24. What is the temperature after it rises by 10°?

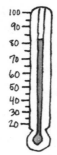

- (F) 97°F
- (G) 92°F
- (H) 90°F
- (J) 88°F

25. Toby left his house for school at 7:35 A.M. He arrived at 7:50 A.M. How many minutes did it take Toby to get to school?

- (A) 15 minutes
- (B) 20 minutes
- (C) 25 minutes
- (D) 10 minutes

26. If there are 12 white socks, 6 black socks, 4 red socks, and 2 purple socks in a drawer, which color are you most likely to pull out without looking?

- (F) white
- (G) black
- (H) red
- (J) purple

27. Rosendo and his sister combine their money to buy a new game. Rosendo has $7.48 and his sister has $8.31. How much money do they have in all?

- (A) $0.83
- (B) $15.79
- (C) $16.89
- (D) Not Here

DIRECTIONS: Use the chart for questions 28–29.

CENTER CINEMAS
MOVIE TICKET SALES

MONDAY
TUESDAY
WEDNESDAY
THURSDAY
FRIDAY

KEY: 10 TICKETS =

28. How many tickets were sold on Wednesday?

- (F) 13.5
- (G) 14
- (H) 135
- (J) 140

29. How many more tickets were sold on Friday than on Tuesday?

- (A) 45
- (B) 55
- (C) 75
- (D) 295

30. One tablespoon holds about 15 milliliters. About how many tablespoons of soup are in a 225-milliliter can?

- (F) 45 tablespoons
- (G) 5 tablespoons
- (H) 3,375 tablespoons
- (J) 15 tablespoons

GO

31. There are 21 fish in every square yard of water in a lake. If the lake is 812 square yards, how many fish are in the lake?

  (A) 17,052
  (B) 23,708
  (C) 29,987
  (D) 14,879

32. The soccer team had $9\frac{1}{2}$ feet of submarine sandwich for their party. They ate 7 feet. Which equation below would you use to find out how much sandwich they had left?

  (F) $9\frac{1}{2} + 7 =$

  (G) $9\frac{1}{2} - 7 =$

  (H) $9\frac{1}{2} \times 7 =$

  (J) $9\frac{1}{2} \div 7 =$

33. Alex is selling chocolate bars for the school band. He sells 2 on the first day, 6 on the second day, and 10 on the third day. If this pattern continues, how many will he sell on the fourth day?

  (A) 20
  (B) 18
  (C) 12
  (D) 14

34. What is the standard form of forty-two thousand nine hundred and one?

  (F) 42,910
  (G) 42,901
  (H) 4,291
  (J) 429,100

35. The only charge to use the pool is the $3.00 parking fee. Which of these number sentences should be used to find how much money the parking lot made on a day when 82 cars were parked there?

  (A) 82 + $3.00 =
  (B) 82 − $3.00 =
  (C) 82 × $3.00 =
  (D) 82 ÷ $3.00 =

36. Look at the problem below. Which of these symbols goes in the circle to get the smallest answer?

  150 ● 6 =

  (F) +
  (G) −
  (H) ×
  (J) ÷

37. Which of these symbols goes in the circle to get the largest answer?

  150 ● 6 =

  (A) +
  (B) −
  (C) ×
  (D) ÷

STOP

Name _____   Date _____

Measurement Test
Answer Sheet

1. (A) (B) (C) (D)
2. (F) (G) (H) (J)
3. (A) (B) (C) (D)
4. (F) (G) (H) (J)
5. (A) (B) (C) (D)
6. (F) (G) (H) (J)
7. (A) (B) (C) (D)
8. (F) (G) (H) (J)
9. (A) (B) (C) (D)
10. (F) (G) (H) (J)

11. (A) (B) (C) (D)
12. (F) (G) (H) (J)
13. (A) (B) (C) (D)
14. (F) (G) (H) (J)
15. (A) (B) (C) (D)
16. (F) (G) (H) (J)
17. (A) (B) (C) (D)
18. (F) (G) (H) (J)
19. (A) (B) (C) (D)
20. (F) (G) (H) (J)

21. (A) (B) (C) (D)
22. (F) (G) (H) (J)
23. (A) (B) (C) (D)
24. (F) (G) (H) (J)
25. (A) (B) (C) (D)
26. (F) (G) (H) (J)
27. (A) (B) (C) (D)
28. (F) (G) (H) (J)
29. (A) (B) (C) (D)
30. (F) (G) (H) (J)

31. (A) (B) (C) (D)
32. (F) (G) (H) (J)
33. (A) (B) (C) (D)
34. (F) (G) (H) (J)
35. (A) (B) (C) (D)
36. (F) (G) (H) (J)
37. (A) (B) (C) (D)

Answer Key

Pages 8–9

1. D
2. J
3. A
4. G
5. C
6. G
7. D
8. G
9. A
10. G
11. C
12. J
13. A
14. G

Pages 10–11

1. C
2. J
3. B
4. H
5. C
6. G
7. A
8. H
9. D
10. H
11. B
12. G
13. D
14. J

Pages 12–13

1. B
2. F
3. D
4. F
5. D
6. G
7. C
8. F

Pages 14–15

1. B
2. G
3. A
4. J
5. A
6. G
7. D
8. F
9. D

Pages 16–17

1. B
2. F
3. C
4. F
5. B
6. F
7. C
8. F
9. S
10. A
11. A
12. S
13. S
14. S
15. S
16. A
17. A
18. S
19. A
20. S

Pages 18–19

1. A
2. J
3. B
4. H
5. C
6. H

Pages 20–21

1. A
2. H
3. B
4. J

Page 22
Mini-Test

1. A
2. G
3. A
4. H
5. D
6. F
7. D

Pages 24–25

1. C
2. F
3. B
4. J
5. A
6. H
7. B
8. F
9. C

Pages 26–27

1. B
2. G
3. A
4. G
5. D
6. G
7. D

Pages 28–29

1. A
2. G
3. C
4. J
5. A
6. G
7. C
8. J

Page 30
Mini-Test

1. B
2. H
3. D
4. F
5. D
6. H

Pages 32–33

1. D
2. G
3. B
4. J
5. A
6. G
7. D
8. H

Pages 34–35

1. A
2. F
3. B
4. G
5. C
6. G

Pages 36–37

1. C
2. G
3. C
4. F
5. C
6. J
7. B
8. C
9. A
10. D
11. C
12. D
13. B
14. A
15. D
16. C
17. B
18. B
19. J

Pages 38–39

1. A
2. H
3. D
4. F
5. C
6. J

Page 40

Mini-Test

1. A
2. H
3. C
4. G
5. C

Pages 42–43

1. B
2. H
3. B
4. H
5. A
6. J
7. B
8. H

Pages 44–45

1. D
2. G
3. C
4. F
5 C

Pages 46–47

1. A
2. G
3. B
4. H
5. D
6. H
7. B

Page 48

Mini-Test

1. A
2. H
3. B
4. H
5. D

Pages 51–54

Final Reading Test

1. D
2. H
3. A
4. H
5. D
6. G
7. D
8. G
9. D
10. G
11. C
12. H
13. B
14. G
15. B
16. G
17. D
18. F
19. B
20. H
21. C
22. F
23. D
24. F
25. A
26. F

Pages 59–60

1. C
2. G
3. D
4. G
5. B
6. H
7. C
8. H
9. C
10. G
11. D
12. F
13. B
14. G
15. C

Pages 61–62

1. C
2. G
3. B
4. G
5. A
6. G
7. C
8. G
9. A
10. J
11. C
12. G
13. C

Pages 63–64

1. A
2. F
3. B
4. G
5. B
6. F
7. D
8. G
9. D
10. H
11. A

Pages 65-66

1. B
2. J
3. B
4. J
5. B
6. J
7. D
8. H

Pages 67–68

1. A
2. J
3. C
4. F
5. D
6. F
7. D
8. F
9. C

Pages 69–70

1. D
2. G
3. C
4. F
5. D
6. H
7. D
8. J
9. B
10. F
11. C
12. H

Pages 71–72

1. A
2. G
3. A
4. G
5. B
6. G
7. D
8. H
9. B
10. J
11. A

Pages 73–74

1. A
2. H
3. B
4. F
5. C
6. J
7. A
8. F
9. C
10. G
11. B
12. J
13. A
14. H
15. B
16. G

Pages 75–76	Pages 77–78	Pages 79–80	Page 81
1. A	**1.** 900; 700; 900; 500; 200; 400; 400; 500; 200	**1.** A	**Mini-Test**
2. H		**2.** G	**1.** C
3. C		**3.** C	**2.** G
4. F		**4.** G	**3.** A
5. B		**5.** D	**4.** G
6. J	**2.** 2,000; 3,000; 4,000; 7,000; 9,000; 6,000; 5,000; 9,000; 3,000	**6.** G	**5.** B
7. A		**7.** A	**6.** H
8. J		**8.** J	**7.** A
9. B		**9.** A	**8.** H
10. F		**10.** J	
11. B		**11.** B	**Pages 83–84**
12. G		**12.** H	**1.** B
13. C		**13.** B	**2.** F
14. F	**3.** B		**3.** C
15. C	**4.** G		**4.** H
16. J	**5.** D		**5.** D
	6. G		**6.** H
	7. B		**7.** C
	8. G		**8.** F
	9. A		**9.** A
	10. F		
	11. 3,000; 2,000; 10,000; 6,000; 5,000; 2,000; 1,000; 5,000; 9,000		
	12. A		

Pages 85–86

1. B
2. H
3. A
4. J
5. Sample answer: 3 circles in 3 groups
6. Sample answer: 6 squares in 1 group
7. Sample answer: 7 triangles in 2 groups
8. Sample answer: 4 stars in 5 groups
9. Sample answer: 6 rectangles in 1 group

Pages 87–88

1. C
2. F
3. D
4. G
5. C
6. F
7. B
8. J
9. A
10. J
11. A
12. G
13. A
14. J
15. B
16. G

Pages 89–90

1. C
2. F
3. A
4. J

Pages 91–92

1. B
2. J
3. C
4. F
5. C

Page 93

Mini-Test

1. C
2. J
3. C
4. H
5. A
6. H

Pages 95–96

1. C
2. H
3. C
4. G
5. A
6. G
7. C
8. J
9. C
10. F
11. C
12. G

Pages 97–98

1. C
2. H
3. C
4. G
5. neither
6. similar
7. congruent
8. similar

Pages 99–100

1. C
2. F
3. D
4. J
5. B
6. H
7. D
8. F

Pages 101–102

1. A
2. H
3. B
4. G
5. D
6. H
7. D
8. F
9. D
10. H
11. B
12. J

Page 103

Mini-Test

1. C
2. J
3. A
4. H
5. D
6. G

Pages 105–106

1. C
2. J
3. B
4. H
5. B
6. H
7. A
8. F
9. B
10. F

Pages 107–108

1. 12 cm
2. 36 in.
3. 89 ft
4. 77 m
5. 65 km
6. 22 in.
7. 84 mm
8. 72 yd
9. 33 m
10. A
11. F
12. A
13. F

Pages 109–110

1. 5
2. 6
3. 6
4. 5; 5
5. 8; 8
6. 12; 12
7. D
8. J
9. B
10. J
11. C

Pages 111–112

1. B
2. H
3. D
4. J
5. A
6. G
7. B
8. J
9. Students should indicate 7:37 on their clocks.

Pages 113–114

1. C
2. H
3. C
4. F
5. B
6. H
7. C

Pages 115–116

1. B
2. J
3. C
4. H
5. D
6. Students should indicate 5:36 on their clocks.
7. G
8. C
9. H
10. C
11. F

Pages 117–118

Mini-Test

1. A
2. H
3. D
4. J
5. C
6. H
7. B
8. H
9. A
10. G
11. B

Pages 120–121

1. C
2. G
3. A
4. H
5. D
6.

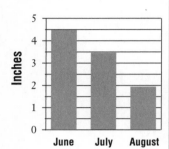

7. Students should create a pictograph that shows the number of boys and girls in their class at school.

Pages 122–123

1. A
2. J
3. B
4. J
5. B
6. H
7. D
8. G

Pages 124–125

1. A
2. J
3. B
4. H
5. C
6. J
7. A
8. J
9. B
10. F
11. B
12. J
13. B
14. J
15. A
16. H

Pages 126–127

Mini-Test

1. B
2. J
3. A
4. H
5. B
6. F
7. B
8. H
9. A
10. F
11. D
12. F

Pages 129–130

1. A
2. H
3. B
4. J
5. C
6. J
7. A
8. H
9. B
10. G
11. B
12. H
13. C

Pages 131–132

1. C
2. F
3. A
4. H
5. D
6. H
7. C
8. J
9. D
10. H

Pages 133–134

1. D
2. F
3. B
4. H
5. D
6. J
7. B
8. F
9. A

Pages 135–136

1. B
2. H
3. D
4. J
5. D
6. J
7. C
8. F
9. B
10. F
11. D
12. F

Pages 137–138

1. D
2. G
3. C
4. G
5. D
6. F
7. 25
8.

①	2	③	4	5̷	6	⑦	8̷	⑨	10
2	4	6	8̷	10	12	1̷4̷	16	18	2̷0̷
③	6	9̷	12	⑮	1̷8̷	㉑	24	2̷7̷	30
4	8̷	12	16	2̷0̷	24	28	3̷2̷	36	40
5̷	10	⑮	2̷0̷	㉕	30	3̷5̷	40	㊺	5̷0̷
6	12	1̷8̷	24	30	3̷6̷	42	48	5̷4̷	60
⑦	1̷4̷	㉑	28	3̷5̷	42	㊼	5̷6̷	㊿	70
8̷	16	24	3̷2̷	40	48	5̷6̷	64	72	80
⑨	18	2̷7̷	36	㊺	5̷4̷	63	72	81	90
10	2̷0̷	30	40	5̷0̷	60	70	80	90	100

9. 7

Page 139

Mini-Test

1. D
2. H
3. B
4. G
5. B
6. F

Pages 142–147

Mathematics

Final Test

1. A
2. F
3. D
4. J
5. D
6. G
7. A
8. H
9. B
10. G
11. B
12. J
13. C
14. G
15. D
16. G
17. D
18. H
19. C
20. H
21. A
22. H
23. C
24. G
25. A
26. F
27. B
28. H
29. B
30. J
31. A
32. G
33. D
34. G
35. C
36. J
37. C